JUST

ANOTHER

DAY

BOBBIE THOMAS PANEK

70 DOWNTOWN
BOOKS
COFFEE
Auburn, NY

Cover photo provided by Mark Gonyea, April 1987.
(My cousin from Malone, NY – my hometown.)

Cover design by John Norman Panek.
(My son.)

For information on this title contact:
Downtown Books Publishing
66 Genesee Street
Auburn, NY 13021
downtownbooksandcoffee.com

ISBN 978-0-692-49408-0

To Greg, Sarah, Laura, Scott & John.

Special thanks to all the farmers who feed the world.

TABLE OF CONTENTS

FOREWORD

Being a twin in a big Irish family with seven sisters we didn't get much individual attention. In parochial school my eighth-grade teacher told me I was a good writer. I loved knowing that I was good at something and that somebody acknowledged that I had a gift.

I wrote journals from the age of twenty and realized that I could then see what I was thinking. When I married a dairy farmer and moved in with him and his Pop, writing became my therapy for dealing with two hard-working Polish men with strong roots to the soil.

Four children later, I bravely marched downtown to *The Citizen* Newspaper Office and asked to write a weekly column. After the editor read a few of my stories, he looked me in the eye and said, "You have a strong voice. You know how to tell a lean story." And he hired me to write a weekly column for the farm section.

Suddenly I was writing a farm blog before blogs were even invented. These 48 stories appeared from April 1988 to April 1989. "Don't Worry, Be Happy," was the most popular song and gas was a whopping ninety-one cents a gallon.

Being a stay-at-home mom for ten years were the best days of my life even though I didn't realize it at the time. I'm grateful to have captured these snippets.

JUST ANOTHER DAY

MEMORIES: THE HANDS OF THE FARMER

William Riester, his hands were huge. When we first met, I naturally glanced at his stature. He was about six feet tall and his 80-year-old frame was showing signs of frailty. I extended my hand to him as a gesture of friendliness and also to make a connection. (The custom of shaking hands with others is a tender, peaceful human tradition that I hope will never cease.) As I extended my hand, he reached out with his. Our eyes said hello, along with our "How do you do?" I felt my hand lost in his. I'd never felt such strength and girth in a handshake.

I'd known a lot of farmers before, but never paid much attention to their hands. Most of the farmers I'd known were my grandfathers, uncles, and cousins. We would all hug hello.

This old gentleman owned a farmhouse with an apartment for rent. I already liked the area: the quiet winding road, the looks of the farm. Now I was in awe of the proprietor.

I moved into the apartment in May, when the bustle of farming was in full throttle. My elderly landlord was still quite active on the farm. He plowed and fitted the fields and, though he did hire someone to harvest for him, was always on site.

He was out early in the morning and would wave and yell "good morning" to me as I was getting into my car. By his side were his constant companions—Duke, a collie, and Kitty, a tiger cat. Together, they would walk out in the fields to supervise the sweet peas, corn, or wheat as it was unloaded into the dryer bin.

One night, I heard the familiar rap on our shared interior door. He came striding through with Duke and Kitty. Pride was apparent on his face as he handed me a pot of fresh, raw, shelled, sweet peas. He bellowed, "Cook these up for the sweetest peas ya ever tasted!" They were delicious cooked but actually I preferred them raw. They were sweet as candy!

One day, I came home from work with a kitten. It was the runt of the litter—copper and white, shy and adorable. I brought the sweet feline through the door connecting our living quarters to introduce my new friend to my old friend. The old man took the scared little creature and cradled it tenderly in his giant paws.

Once again, I marveled at his hands. They were the hands of a farmer, laborer, husband, father, grandfather, and friend. And now that he was widowed and alone, those hands did housework as well.

He helped me nurture tomato plants that we grew from seed that he kept by a sunny window. When it was time to transplant them, he used his cane to point to each spot in the garden where the plant should go.

When his eyes twinkled, I knew he was going to tell a story. His wealth of knowledge about farming and local history and keen sense of humor often surfaced in his storytelling. He would laugh loudly at his own jokes. When he sighed, he'd let out a cavernous roar.

The first time I saw him sitting at his old sewing machine and patching his own work pants, I was shocked. I could barely use a sewing machine and here was this old man doing such intricate work.

I must admit, the thing about him I liked best were his home-made apple pies. He made them with his own loving hands.

William Riester died one winter morning. He is gone now, yet I think his spirit will live forever.

CONTEST GOES BEYOND THE FIRST ROBIN

Which one of us will be the first to see a robin this year? As winter turns to spring, we have a contest on the farm to see who will see the red-breasted bird.

My husband has won most often. He is outside a great deal and is quite observant. One year I won the contest. How I relished that glorious feeling of triumph.

What's interesting is how the winner resembles a robin for a couple of days. The person's chest gets slightly inflated, his head cocked a little to one side and his walk a bit more like a strut.

Two years ago, our eight-year-old daughter saw a robin before the rest of us. We were in the kitchen eating breakfast when Sarah exclaimed, "A robin!" We all looked out the west window to see a big, fat, beautiful bird perched on the tree. He waited long enough for each of us to get a good look at him, and then flew off to spread the news of his arrival around the neighborhood.

Last year, I was intent on being the winner. I don't know why it was so important to me but I continuously looked out the west window of our kitchen to scan the yard for the friendly bird. I felt that with my rapt vigil I had a good chance.

One morning, my two sons and I went for a stroll down the street. We visited with neighbors while spring fever permeated our senses. The air felt fresh and fragrant.

On the way home, my four-year-old son ran through the back yard of our farm while I continued down the road and up the driveway with my toddler in the stroller.

We met at the sidewalk and walked into the house together. Soon after, my husband came in and said, "Hey, I saw Scotty in the back yard trying to catch a bird. Was it a robin?"

I ran to the east window to look. Sure enough, the herald of spring was strutting on the lawn. I yelled, "Yeah! I saw him first." My husband quickly pointed out that Scotty won the contest.

I said, "But that doesn't count because he didn't KNOW it was a robin!" Then I felt a little silly for trying to take the glory away from a four-year-old.

I looked at Scotty proudly and said, "You did it, Scott! You saw the first robin this year." A smile spread across his face, his little chest puffed up and he began to prance around the room.

I made an award out of construction paper and taped it on the kitchen wall. When Scott's sisters got home from school, they saw the award and cheered: "Wow, Scott, good for you!"

I learned a thing or two. I thought about how often I'd looked out the wrong window for the bird and couldn't help but wonder if that's a common thread with people keeping a narrow vision when being open to other ideas might be more fruitful.

Oh well, that was last year. As for this year, "Let the games begin!" I don't get much work done now, running back and forth in the kitchen between the east and west windows.

P.S. A few days later, seven-year-old Laura won! She was looking out the picture window and all of a sudden let out a proud, delightful scream.

I'm happy for her. Honest. Really.

IT WAS A BLACK, WHITE, AND GRAY DAY

Spring unpacked but forgot a few things. She went back for another paintbrush and some more paint. And she left us with nasty winter who is getting in some final blows.

One of our black and white Holstein cows became ill last week. She lay on the barn floor, too weak to get up. The antibiotic didn't cure her and today we had to call the rendering service to come and get her. It was sad to see her go like that, but better than watching her suffer.

After the rendering truck left, we went to the dump. What a sight, driving along the deeply rutted road to giant heaps of garbage.

I sat in the pickup truck, staring at the contrasts around us. Beautiful, elegant sea gulls feasted on the garbage. The birds were stark white and silver gray with jet black wing tips, looking proud and dignified while they picked through refuse. Streamlined and smooth, they took off and landed with little effort.

Later at home I heard a—CLUNK! I could tell from the sound that a bird had just crashed into our picture window. Our bird feeder is close to the window. Once in a while, a bird tries to fly through the glass to get to the bird feeder's reflection.

When I looked outside, a pretty little gray, black and white chickadee sat motionless on the sidewalk. Its head moved slightly but I thought it was probably suffering internal damage. Then I saw the cat.

"Oreo Cookie," our black and white barn cat, was within two feet of the bird. Fine snowflakes began to fall on the two animals.

Oreo watched the bird intently for any sign of movement. I figured that the cat was going to pounce on the bird quickly. Hopefully, the bird would soon be out of its misery. I didn't want to watch anymore, but the drama of the scene kept me pinned to the couch, staring out the window.

Slowly, very slowly, Oreo stalked the little bird. The cat acted timid and confused, not quite sure why the bird didn't fly away. He sniffed the ground beside the bird, and then sniffed the little animal. His paw nudged the chickadee, who barely moved. The cat acted so tender that, for a fleeting moment, I thought that maybe the cat would befriend the little bird. But then Oreo's paw made a sweeping motion. It must have been the necessary motivation to arouse the bird from its stupor. Aloft—the bird was up. It flew away!

Snow continued to fall on the black and white cat as he sat staring at the gray sky.

BLOOMING MARIGOLDS

'Seems like Martin's rooster is crowing earlier and earlier,' thought Dorothy as she got out of bed. 'Hmm… This will be a good day to start my marigolds.'

She ate breakfast, washed the dishes, and then climbed up to the attic to find the plastic plant beds she'd used so many times. Dorothy liked them because of their individual compartments. With a lively step, she carried them downstairs to the kitchen.

Growing marigolds from seeds was one of Dorothy's favorite spring projects. She had fond memories of poking the seeds down into the potting soil with her chubby little-girl fingers as she sat with her mother and sister, Sal. Now her fingers were thin and frail, but the thrill was the same.

Before beginning her project, Dorothy turned on the radio. She and Perry Como sang *Find a Wheel* in perfect harmony while she got everything ready: a bag of soil, a package of seeds, plastic trays, and a roasting pan—time to begin.

She sat down at the kitchen table, placed a tray on the roasting pan, and then opened the bag of soil. A wonderful earthy smell escaped into the room. Dorothy smiled.

She put her hand into the bag, scooped a palm full of the rich humus and filled each tray with nutritious soil. Then, she carefully opened the marigold package, poured some seeds into her hand and put two in each compartment. One might hope that each seed would perform perfectly, but Dorothy knew that some seeds refuse to grow, while others produce less than perfect flowers. Even that was okay. Each flower that grew would be special.

When all the seeds were pushed below the soil, she carefully watered the trays and set them in her bay window, where the morning sun felt warm and wonderful. Every day that followed, her neighbor's rooster crowed earlier and earlier, until the marigold sprouts were baby plants with buds on them.

Dorothy transplanted them outside in flower boxes by her front door. Each summer, her neighbors and friends commented on their beauty. My friend rejoiced knowing that her flowers made the world just a little bit prettier.

Blind from birth, Dorothy had never seen a marigold. She could feel their fullness of petals and could smell their strong golden scent. She had been told they were the color of the sun, and she'd certainly felt the warmth and wonder of that.

FAMILY VISIT
MEMORABLE AND MUDDY

My younger sister Maryclaire came to visit us, to see her nieces and nephews and to breathe country air. She enjoys getting away from the concrete city of Washington, DC There's something about rural America that settles the soul and soothes the spirit.

After a big lunch, checking out photo albums, and much talking and reminiscing, we decided to go for a walk. It was a cold day so my father-in-law loaned us his big warm jackets. Maryclaire covered her chic coat with Pop's hooded sweatshirt and tattered quilted vest. She looked quite *country*. I borrowed Pop's big red parka. The children bundled up. Even with all of our layered clothing, we still felt the cold April wind.

We walked across the plowed field to the pond. I took a picture of Maryclaire and the children huddled among a family of willow trees. We looked for the uninvited muskrat that has taken up residence in our pond, but we couldn't find him. We did find a pair of ducks sitting by the cultivator. When the mallards saw us approach, they quickly slid into the water. I walked along one side of the pond to take a picture of the pair as they glided effortlessly across the water. I was unaware that my daughters were on the other side of the pond, gliding effortlessly into deep trouble.

Laura got stuck in the black mud that my husband had recently dug out of the creek. There are many different kinds of mud on the farm. We have barnyard mud, casual driveway mud, field mud, and creek mud. Creek mud is the blackest, slimiest and stickiest! Laura got stuck real bad or real good; in either case about half of her body was above ground.

I heard everybody yell for me, so I headed back to the group to see what was up. Right about then, Maryclaire, who was wearing sneakers, sent Sarah, who was wearing boots, to help Laura. That is when Sarah got stuck.

Everybody else was laughing. I didn't. After all, I do the laundry. And I had yet to put away two loads of clothes from that morning.

Maryclaire was able to reach over to pull Sarah's hand. Sarah fell to the knees of her new off-white slacks trying to get free.

I was the lucky one who had to rescue Laura. Walking to her was tricky. I found a big rock and laid it down as a stepping stone. It worked as my first step. I saw a piece of brush for my second step. After that, I was on my own. I placed my foot on the highest bump of mud hoping that it was a little dry. My foot sank to China.

I pulled Laura out by the hand. Her body moved toward me. That is, her body, legs and feet moved towards me, but her boots stayed where they were.

The sounds of merriment twittered all around me. I was getting a headache. One at a time, Laura's baby-blue socked feet flew out from her boots and landed smack in the middle of creek muck. Liberated, Laura muddled toward the hysterical crew while I yanked her boots from their hold.

My right foot was still perched precariously on its little island in the sea of mud. My left foot was nowhere to be seen. I struggled to free myself and finally managed to pull my leather hiking boot out of the mire. It had once been such a nice light brown...

Laura's yellow parka was very muddy, her socks were no longer discernible and, as I tried pulling the soggy things off her feet, she fell against me and wiped black sludge all over Pop's red parka. Naturally, that brought more giggles.

Walking back to the house, Maryclaire apologized for contributing to the laugh track, and I apologized for being such a stick-in-the-mud. She admitted that she is so used to the sidewalks and pavement in the city that being in the country muck was novel and fun. I told her that I was surprised at her reaction with all of the mud-slinging in Washington, DC

I kept reminding myself as I washed load after load of laundry, it was good to see my sister. And we did have a memorable day we're not likely to forget anytime soon.

A PLEA ON BEHALF OF ABUSED CHILDREN

I had a lovely story for today written recently on a rainy morning. The soft green lawns were a watercolor. Lilac, blue and pink hyacinths waxed from the rain. I wanted to share the moment when I saw a brilliant red cardinal sitting in our rich yellow forsythia bush. The article focused on birds frolicking on our lawn, about planted oat fields, and box elder trees as proud parents with newborn leaves.

Then I worked at the polls on Tuesday as an Election Inspector at the Herman Avenue School and knew I wanted to write about the beauty of the children who walked the halls instead. This time of year, tulips are breathtaking: but they cannot compare to the landscape of innocence. The images of freckled noses, brush cuts, frosted jean jackets, and pants with worn-out knees all seemed more important.

A little girl came skipping down the corridor as though she were in a musical. Her blond hair fanned out around her angelic face as she glided to music that only she could hear. She stopped when she realized that I was watching her. I stared at her despite myself, mesmerized by her happiness. When she turned the corner, she resumed her merry gait. Ah, to be young! I have never seen an adult skip like that.

Children walked in and out of their classrooms following their teachers like baby chicks following their mother. Two little girls in pastel skirts held hands and giggled about a shared secret. Some boys walked by in GI Joe outfits. Others more preppie had turned up their alligator shirt collars.

3 o'clock was when the halls were really bustling. Children ambled out, some tired, some sad, some bouncy. Some ran when their teachers weren't watching. It wasn't long before we realized that the snacks on our table were causing some distressed looks among them. What child isn't hungry right after school? We removed our snacks from view and were relieved to see more children smile.

I made a conscious decision to write about the beauty of children rather than the beauty of spring. However, something changed my plans for this column.

I came home from the polls and my husband, Greg, and I sat and talked about our day. He was busy with field work and caring for our four children. I had a lot to share about my day. As we sat talking, a PBS television program called "The Unquiet Deal of Eli Creekmore" grabbed our attention. To quote The Citizen's TV guide, the program "examined the issue of child abuse through the case of a three-year-old boy who was beaten to death by his father."

I won't go into detail about the story. I can't. The horror is too intense. The blond-haired, blue-eyed, adorable, vulnerable little boy was repeatedly beaten. I had to leave the room unable to watch any more of that true story. I sat on my bed, rocked back and forth, and cried and cried. Feeling painfully helpless, I cried for all the children in the world who are abused and prayed with my whole heart to be able to DO something—anything--to help.

So I changed my story for today to include a plea to the world. This is something I had to put in words, organize in sentences, and see on paper.

Children don't ask to be born. They arrive here ready to absorb what experiences the world offers. Please help them. Guide and nurture them. Cherish their joys and understand their sorrows. I'm not qualified to beg people to get help if they need it. I don't know what words to use. I only know what is in my heart. If you are abusing a child, please stop. If you suspect someone of abusing a child, please report that person. We can all DO something.

Children are God's greatest gifts.

WHO'S COUNTING CHICKENS ANYWAY?

I knew the day would be interesting when I found 2 ½-year-old Johnny with his hand in the peanut butter jar. Actually, it was his hand and half his arm--the big jar was nearly empty.

After getting Johnny all cleaned up, he rode along while I drove Sarah, Laura, and Scott to school. One of them forgot to bring some homework home, so I took them in early.

We dropped them off them off at school, and then we went to Agway for some supplies. We were thrilled to see three varieties of downy, three-week-old chicks in two big tubs. The soft, feathery, little birds crowded on the floor of the tubs, where they were kept warm with heat lamps. We admired their busy antics and flurry of movement. They were two for $1, and I had a strong urge to buy at least two. Baby chicks peep so sweetly and their eyes are so bright. I resisted the urge to buy them because I wasn't sure if we had the proper equipment to care for them that night.

I've always wanted to raise a few chickens. I've especially wanted a rooster. What a great sound at day break: "Cock-a-doodle doo!" Our friends have roosters and I can even hear them crowing over the phone.

When Johnny and I returned to the farm, we saw Pop outside waiting for us. He wanted us to go with him to an implement dealer. On the way, I told him about the baby chicks and how I wanted to buy four of them. Suddenly two didn't seem like enough; we should get one for each of our children. Pop found the idea somewhat acceptable, fueling my thoughts.

At the dealers, Johnny immediately climbed on the child-size tractor. It sits there for children to play with and Johnny knew right where to find it. When it was time to go I had to literally peel him off the tractor. He loves the whole gamut of farm equipment: tractors, trucks, planters, plows, and combines.

When we returned home, we busied ourselves outside washing lawn chairs and getting out the homemade bench that Greg had fashioned from a long wooden plank on top of two painted five-gallon oil cans.

Greg was out disking fields and I got impatient to hear his thoughts on getting a few baby chicks, so Johnny and I walked across the recently planted oat field, past the pond, along the hay field, to the plowed field where he was disking. He stopped when he saw us and we climbed up into the cab.

Johnny sat on his Dad's lap and I squished next to them. Half of me was on the arm of the chair and half was on the window ledge. The ride was bumpy. Every time we hit a plowed furrow, which was *constantly*, we all flew up in the air. Greg and Johnny always landed on the softly padded seat. I never knew where I'd land.

To my surprise, when I mentioned getting four chickens Greg said, "Why not eight?" Wow, our chickens were multiplying already!

As soon as I got Greg to agree to my "baby chick" plan, Johnny and I climbed down. Getting Johnny off the big tractor was even harder than getting him off the tiny tractor at the dealer's.

I decided to wait to go back to Agway. The following day was Saturday and I wanted our children to help with adopting our new farm members.

At breakfast, Pop had changed his tune and tried to talk me out of getting the chickens. My ears, however, were listening to a distant "cock-a-doodle-doo."

The kids and I drove off in quest of feathered friends. What fun we had trying to catch the little creatures. We all stood at one end of the tub and, just as we reached down to pick one up, in a flutter of activity they all scrambled to the other end of their haven. This continued until we outsmarted them, divided our troops, and stood at both ends of the big tank. Finally we had eight--a combination of the varieties.

When we arrived home we put them in a big box. Guess who seemed to like them the most? Pop! He reminded Greg of the brooder that was in the attic. Grandma Panek had always raised 50 chicks each spring and the brooder was still in great shape.

Greg and Sarah carried the parts downstairs and outside. They cleaned it off, assembled it, and we put our eight downy friends into their new condo in our back room.

Pop said, "They've got so much room in there, too bad you didn't get 10."

Greg said, "Why don't you go back and make it an even dozen?"

So, the girls and I went back to Agway for four more but we lost count … and came back with six.

Now the 14 baby chicks are happy as can be in their own little house and we all run around like mother hens attending to their needs.

How soon will the roosters crow? I'll let you know!

TRUE HAPPINESS: CHICKENS IN THE BARN

I have found the way to true happiness, and you can too! All you have to do is buy 14 baby chicks, put them in a brooder in the back room of your house, keep them there for 10 days, and then (drum roll) move them to the barn. INSTANT HAPPINESS!

I guarantee you absolute, total joy. Our fast growin,' squawkin', scratchin,' foul smellin', feather-flyin' chickens are now in the barn and I am elated. They will enjoy their new spacious home and I will certainly enjoy a chicken-free house. My sinuses were working overtime.

The experience reminds me of a story I once read. I can't remember the author or the title, but the gist of the story goes something like this:

There was a man named Pete. He lived in a tiny, one-room hut with his wife, their 14 children and his mother and father-in-law. Pete was very unhappy. The cramped quarters, odors and dirt floor were wearing on him. He decided to take his problem to a wise old hermit who lived high up on a mountain. Pete climbed for hours to reach the peak and finally found the guru sitting on a cliff. Frustrated Pete told the wise man about his plight. The teacher told Pete what to do.

He said, "Get a goat. Tie it to a peg in your dirt floor. Leave it there for one week, then come back to me!"

Pete did as he was instructed. He bought a goat, brought it to his very crowded one-room home and tied it to a peg. The smell of the goat and its droppings were positively horrible. The week passed and Pete could barely wait to go back to the teacher.

When Pete returned to the mountain peak, the wise man told him to leave the goat tied to the peg for one more week and then come back. Pete reluctantly did as he was told and was most unhappy with the crowded, smelly situation.

Finally, the second week ended and the man practically ran up the mountain to see what the prophet had to say.

The hermit told Pete, "Now go home and sell the goat and you will be very happy!" Indeed, Pete was jubilant. He thanked the teacher for his solution and ran down the mountain. He sold the goat immediately and settled back into his home. Pete and all of the family members were as happy as they could be.

This is one of my favorite stories. I read it several years ago and never forgot its simple truth. "Be content with the way things are; things could be worse."

If you don't believe me, tie an elephant to your refrigerator door for one week.

While you're seeking inner peace, I will enjoy visiting our chickens in the barn and still look forward to that early morning cock-a-doodle-doo!

MEMORY OF SPUDS: A CALL TO FORK

To plant potatoes or not ... that's the question. Last May, while we were planting sweet corn, string beans, tomatoes and carrots, our youngest daughter Laura asked, "Can we plant potatoes too? I love it when we have our own potatoes to eat; when we can walk outside, dig them up, and fix them for supper."

I found her comments interesting. As the one who, while starting supper preparations, would have to change into my boots, run out to the garden, forget the pitchfork, remember the pitchfork, run to the barn to find a pitchfork, head to the garden again, dig up a few hills of potatoes, carry the dirt-covered 'taters' home, clean off the lumps of dirt, bring them in the house, change back to my shoes, then peel or scrub them, I always found ripping open a store-bought 10-pound bag so much easier.

Laura's remarks got us all salivating for homegrown potatoes. Greg and I looked at each other and agreed, "Yeah, let's plant potatoes again."

Greg brought a bushel of seed potatoes home and on the following weekend, when my sister's family visited from the Adirondacks, we cut potatoes to plant.

My twin sister Beckie and I sat in lawn chairs in the sun with a bushel of potatoes in two bags on either side of us and sharp knives in our hands. We talked and laughed and watched our children, as we cut the potatoes making sure there were at least two eyes on each cut section. Then, we placed the cut piece in the little red wagon between our chairs.

A few days later, when the potatoes were cured and the garden was eagerly waiting, the kids and I followed Greg to the garden. He led with his hoe.

When Greg had dug the first two trenches, Laura pulled the handle of the wagon between the rows and five-year-old Scott pushed it along. Sarah, our nine-year-old, and I bent over each row raced to complete our furrows.

Grandpa pushed Johnny in the stroller and they watched from the sidelines as we planted the cut spuds.

The weather that day was ideal. It was warm and a little cloudy, so the sun didn't beat too harshly on us. We raced and laughed and worked. Together we kicked over the soil and stomped on each row to settle the earth above the big seeds.

Within a couple of hours, the bushel of cut potatoes was firmly in place and we marched back to the house, our steps still lively after all our work.

Keeping the planted seeds hilled during the summer was a chore for my husband and me when we were in the mood. But digging up the clusters of new spuds in the fall was the clincher.

We decided that the children should help us with the harvest, since they were willing participants from the start. Weeds had moved in on those sultry summer days, making it difficult to even find some of the potato plants. On this autumn day, the sun beat down on us and sweat trickled down our necks. The barn cats all wanted to help. They played around our feet and did a great job of keeping the children distracted. Instead of picking up the dug-potatoes they were picking up cats.

Walking a mile in their shoes made us appreciate the farmers who give us quality vegetables that have been graded, cleaned, and packaged.

Our potatoes sure tasted good. Soon, our sore backs were forgotten. Hmmm...maybe we ought to plant them again next year.

THE BIRDS, THE WIND WILL STILL BE HERE

I'm sitting in the sun and wind while 2 ½ year-old Johnny is nearby playing in the sandbox. Topaz the cat is meandering around.

A few minutes ago I was hanging clothes on the clothesline and Johnny was sitting on the swing watching me. He yelled over to me "Hope a blackbird doesn't come and snap off your nose Mom." How thoughtful of him to worry about me.

Johnny and I are listening to birds tell stories in the trees. We hear the roar of an airplane in the distance. Wind slaps at the papers of my notebook and causes them to hit my arm with a musical sound.

Today is the Friday before Memorial Day. People drive by our house on their way to the cemetery to decorate graves. This will be a busy day for traveling. Another airplane groans above as a yellow school bus passes.

I think how, when this farm was settled years ago there were no airplanes, buses or cars. But they had the birds and the wind just as we do now.

Greg's out spraying corn. Pops is roller--harrowing another field, getting it ready for planting. There are a lot of steps to growing a crop. When I first married a dairy farmer, I naively thought that all you had to do was plow, plant and harvest. I've learned that there's a lot more to it. First, you drain-tile to get rid of excess water, then you plow, disk, roller--harrow, plant, cultipack to firm and pulverize with a corrugated roller, and spray. Wait. Then harvest.

Some of the corn is about four inches high. The long rows of little green blades change daily. It's fun to watch fields change as the crops grow. You don't need a calendar if you've planted corn. The different heights, colors and stages of development tell you the time of the year.

Fields of oats are especially enjoyable to watch. They often look like green-blue seas. A soft wind makes them ripple in waves. Their color ranges from green to aquamarine, beige, bright yellow and bleached gold.

And wheat is the basis for so much of our food. When I see fields of golden grains swaying in the breeze, I become inspired.

I want to savor these days, make each one last. What a great time of year. I could talk about our peonies that have yet to open, about the thrill of picking wild raspberries, about haying time right around the corner, but I don't want to think beyond this moment.

The sun feels so warm and the birds are all talking at the same time. They have so much to say. Johnny is totally absorbed in a coffee can filled with water and sand that he's stirring with a little stick.

Oh hello, little butterfly! He just dipped and flew right in front of me. There's a big mosquito. Keep on going, fella.

Where did the school year go? Our kids will be out soon. It's nearly time for long days spent outside playing croquet, swimming, and haying.

Later in the day David Grunfeld comes over to take a picture of me 'on the farm'. He has me stand in the doorway of our old barn. Its wood has been weathered a long, long time. Its windows are empty spaces. It creaks and sways and has seen a lot more than me in its seventy-five years.

After lunch, the county crew installs a new drainage pipe on the roadside in front of our house. Johnny and I sit in lawn chairs and watch in fascination as the Gradall excavator moves like a dinosaur, biting into chunks of soil and asphalt. The machine is big and looks clumsy, but moves with agility and precision. Johnny and I are both entranced with the invention.

This is just another day on the farm. I'm enjoying this moment but am reminded of the past by the old barn and intrigued by the future. What comes after airplanes, school busses, and excavators?

I don't know. But the birds and the wind will still be here.

STOP TO SEE THE
PETALS ON THE PETUNIAS

At 7:30 a.m., the phone rang. Our neighbor Penny said, "The ducklings started to hatch last night. When I looked at them this morning, they were on their way to the creek." I quickly put the camcorder together and called the three older children, who scrambled out of pajamas and into clothes. We ran across the street, through the oat fields, to the creek. We met Penny and her three-year-old daughter, Erin. They were looking over the bank for the traveling band of mallards.

A pair of ducks had adopted our little pond as their home. Last month, Penny showed us where the female duck laid a dozen eggs in a nest beside her house. We looked forward to the end of the 30-day period. I asked Penny to let me know when the ducks hatched because I wanted to tape a movie of their trek to the pond. The pond feeds a creek that runs behind Penny's house. The Mama with her fluffy offspring walked to the creek and headed east for the pond. By the time we found them they had traveled about 200 feet, about half-way to their destination.

The children, Penny, and I were thrilled at the sight. The babies followed their mom with absolute determination. Some were just one-day-old taking this journey. They went down a steep bank into cool creek water, paddled upstream, around rocks, roots and branches. A piece of plywood obstructed a section of the creek but they managed to swim under it.

Then, they reached a major hurdle. Many big and small rocks were piled up along the side of the bridge. These ducks weren't rock climbers! The Mama started to quack loudly. She knew we were nearby and she felt nervous and under pressure. How was she going to get her babies to the pond? Daddy duck quickly came to her aid. All of this time, he'd been swimming in the pond, waiting to welcome his family. Now, he swooped close to our heads and landed very near in the cornfield. His brilliant color, noisy quack and proximity to us were meant to keep us more interested in him than the newborns. And it worked.

We backed away from the bank and enjoyed the male's antics. Meanwhile, Mama tried to figure out which way to go. Finally she led her charming dark brown and yellow babies through the foot-tall grass and up the steep bank. The Daddy flew over and acted as a crossing guard as the Mom and her little darlings waddled across the lane and paddled safely into the pond.

What a thrill for us. We were enthralled. We all held hands and said a quick prayer thanking God for letting us share in such a joyous moment and we prayed for the safety of this feathered family.

Of course, not every day can be quite that "ducky" -- but this time of the year is so full of happenings. Wild and domestic animals, plants, flowers, trees are all performing their individual drama. There's so much to enjoy, appreciate, and applaud. And yet the summer often tumbles by. I feel like going outside very early some June morning and shouting at the top of my lungs, "Slow down!"

Swoosh! The summer always seems to pass with lightning speed. We get so wrapped up with graduations, weddings, and reunions, that we often miss the subtle, simple yet intricate designs in nature. Maybe if there were large numbers of people outside their houses on the same day and if we all yelled, "Slow down!" at the same time, maybe June would throw herself into a lower gear.

However, it might not work. Perhaps we'd have better luck if we chose to "slow us down." If we made sure to take time out between our busy scheduled activities to ponder a pond, to study a nearby creek, pick some wildflowers, admire poppies as they change from their fuzzy to papery stage, we'd appreciate the charm and power of the season. If we took more walks in a field, the woods, down the street or on a country road, we'd notice more than we ever could while driving by in a car. We'd smell pine trees, fields of cut hay, barbecued food. We'd hear people living outside the boundaries of their homes.

If we make a conscious point every day to enjoy nature's immeasurable beauty and look closely at the petals of petunias, listen dearly to the concerts of crickets, and let fireflies light up our lives then, when summer comes to a screeching halt, we won't find ourselves saying, "Where did it go?"

PIONEERING SPIRIT

One recent June evening, our family piled into our station wagon and went for a ride in "the big country." Funny how far you have to drive to get there! What used to be farmlands are now rows of houses. An old one-room schoolhouse is now part of a large home. Barns once used for raising livestock and for holding feed are now leaning monuments to their busy past.

We passed varied houses displaying different styles and tastes. There was a quaint brick house, a log cabin with an inviting front porch, a new modern house with cathedral windows and an old Victorian homestead that had been restored.

I understand that development is important. People need shelter. New houses add to the economic base of a town. But it sure does change the scenery. Of course, we have options if we want to live where it's rural. We can just keep on moving away from developed land; that is, until we bump into the development coming from the other direction.

What was most fun about our country ride was reaching the small farm of our friends Bill and Kathy, who are a bit like pioneers. Their farmhouse is at least 100 years old and they're gradually renovating it. They've saved the wooden spindles from their front porch and plan to refinish them and use them once again for the porch railing.

Bill is a logger and has his own sawmill. Up in the barn is the frame for a house that Bill has hand-hewn from big red pine logs. The frame is solid and strong and quite impressive even lying on the barn floor.

Kathy was spreading manure on the horse pasture when we arrived. She and Bill bought a used McCormick spreader. They'd worked on it that afternoon to get it in smooth operating condition. When Kathy climbed down from the tractor to greet us, I had to smile at the smudges on her face and shirt and at the dirt on her hands. She's such a pretty lady when she's all spiffed up and here she was, looking rugged and proud.

It's their spirit that makes me happy. They're keeping a small farm going by sheer determination. They have a big vegetable garden, some old rose bushes that Kathy tends, a giant maple shading their front lawn and they continue to eke out their lives on a well-weathered farm.

Another friend Mary, who has her own farm with numerous animals, inspires me. She milks her one cow every other day. The Jersey keeps her supplied with fresh, rich milk. Mary has a Mama goat named Honeysuckle. And Honeysuckle recently gave birth to two kids, Doc and Buttercup. Two dogs, a horse, a mule, a cat and some chickens round off Mary's family.

Francine, another dear friend, amazes me with her talents. She gutted, insulated, put up drywall, built a deck, and renovated her old house all by herself. I'm glad that we still have people like them around. We need reminders of how it can be. Don't you just love their pioneering spirit?

HAYING IS A CHALLENGING SPORT

Haying is a neglected sport. There's much ado about tennis, golf and baseball but what about haying? It's a true-blue sport and it's about time it gained recognition.

Haying allows you to exercise many muscles, is good for cardiovascular fitness, makes you sweat, and gets adrenaline pumping through your body so you feel like a well-tuned engine. The sport is competitive and fun.

When you are done playing, instead of looking at the scoreboard or counting your strokes you just look in the barn at the stacks of bales and you know you've won.

The smell of sweet hay is exhilarating. Granted, you do get some of the dust up your nose, but that's OK. Have you smelled a locker room or dugout lately?

Equipment is simple. Rather than a racket, club or bat, all you need is a steel hook in the shape of a question mark, with a wooden handle. Attire is simple too. Forget the white shorts, alligator shirts and uniforms. All you need are jeans, T-shirt and old sneaks. The barn is your playing field, the wagon your court. You are ready to begin.

Once you get accustomed to the game, you'll use your body as momentum to handle bales with agility and grace.

I work from the wagon and my husband, Greg, works up on in the mow. I unload the bales onto an elevator. Greg takes them off the elevator and stacks them four high. He has the harder job but I would never admit that to him.

It's easier in the early stage of the game when the barn is empty enough for a wagon to be driven right inside. With the big doors open wide air breezes in and out, and you're shaded from the hot sun.

Above the musical rattle of the elevator, Greg and I have fun banter. We kid each other about being too slow. Sometimes, I speed up bales just to hear him holler, "Slow-down!" Other times, when I'm really hustling on the wagon he yells, "C'mon, can't you go any faster?"

When you think of backhand strokes in tennis, sand traps in golf and poor pitches in baseball, you have to expect some challenges in haying. For instance, a broken bale in the middle of the wagon can fan loose hay in so many directions it'll trip you up and slow you down and could even make you curse, if you were the cursin' type.

There's strategy involved, too. Sometimes, when the wagon is half empty, there's a haphazard wall of bales. This is when you eye the situation and instinctively figure which bale to pull out. If you figured right, about 10 bales will fly right to the foot of the elevator.

Late in the season when the barn is nearly full, the pressure of our game feels like Wimbledon, the Pro Am, or the World Series. The wagon is out in the blazing sun on a hill. The lucky one on the wagon (*moi*) has to pull bales uphill to the elevator. And Greg is high up in the mow where it's so hot, there's very little air. That's when you work your body to its limits.

The good news is you don't have to be a member of a farm-team to play. This summer, on your way to the tennis court or golf course, just stop by at the farm nearest you and ask if they'll let you play haying. With luck, they'll have an extra hook.

I'm sure most farmers would let you play for about two bucks a wagon, maybe three wagons for five bucks. So go ahead and have a bale!

Who knows? Maybe there will be "Haying" in the '92 Summer Olympics!

OLD BARN HOLDS
ALL KINDS OF FEELINGS

Nestled in a valley on a quiet country road is a farm. The buildings are dark red, the lawns are manicured. White fences define flower beds of red geraniums and yellow marigolds. Two German Shepherds greet me as a fat tabby wanders away.

A sprawling maple tree stretches its arms over the yard, offering shade and shelter. Its leaves rustle like chimes in the wind. A white iron pump on the front lawn is not only pretty but functional. With just a few pumps, it makes a lovely screeching sound and cool, clean drinking water gushes out.

There's a tall, narrow smokehouse behind the house, fashioned from reddish pink bricks. Two red painted doors lend a charming atmosphere. Years ago, a pig would hang in there and the smoke rising up from hickory logs would flavor and cure the meat. A chicken house and wagon house border a garden which boasts long, lush rows of potatoes, onions, tomatoes, and other well-nurtured vegetables.

A small milk house holds a box cooler with two lids that stored cans of fresh milk. On the walls are racks that held the milk pails while they drained.

Amid all of this calm, old setting stands a barn. To get into the lower portion where the cows were housed, I walk under a low doorway. Once inside the cave-like structure, stories and silent echoes are heard. But where are the cows? I can almost hear the gentle mooing of Holsteins and the rattle of stanchions as if cows were shifting in their stalls. I can easily imagine heaps of green hay and smell the sweet aroma of grain.

Sun sneaks in windows and plays artist on the white-washed stone walls. Steel stanchions create shadows like soldiers standing at attention. Hundreds of stones piled on top of each other form the craggy foundation walls. I envision men and women bending to put the stones in place one by one.

Solid, strong, round logs stretch across the ceiling, making me feel safe and secure in the area below. A wooden ladder on one wall leads up to a chute in the ceiling where hay was forked down from the mow to the cows below. A bird's nest on one of the log beams tells me that barn swallows still call this their home. Though the barn has not been used for almost twenty years, a cow could walk right in and feel at home.

I feel transposed to another country. I could be in a barn in France, Germany, Poland or Holland. There is a universal aura about this home for cows.

If I went into the farmhouse, I would see clues of the language spoken, and fabrics of the culture. I would be able to tell what country I was in. But here, chiseled into the earth, was an eloquent old barn waiting for silence to cease.

A WALK IN THE WOODS VS. STAYING HOME

We decided to go for a walk on the nature trail at the college. It was a hot summer morning, about 80 degrees in the shade, and a walk in the cool woods seemed like a good idea.

My neighbor Sue and I went to the trail in quest of cool surprises in the woods. We brought with us eight children whose ages spanned one to 10 years. What could possibly go wrong?

Soon after we hit the trail, a big German Shepherd joined our ranks. He decided that we needed his hot, wet body weaving in and out of our legs and in front of the stroller. The dog loved the picturesque ponds. He jumped in all of them. Each time, we had to act quickly to get eight children out of range as he shook pond water in a zillion directions.

Not too far from the beginning of the one-mile loop, Mike, one of the three-year-olds told me how tired he was; his feet couldn't go another step. So, I picked him up and carried him on my hip. A little sweat trickled down my face; no big deal, but it did tickle and I almost tripped over the dog.

My 2 ½- year-old Johnny was running along happily when he saw me carrying the three-year-old. He instantly decided that if his mom was going to carry a little boy, then it had to be him. Fortunately, Sue saved the crisis. She took over carrying Mike, so I could pick up Johnny.

The "cool shady wood" was actually a very wide path with the sun beating down. There were tiny patches of shade now and then. We were sweaty, but all was fine…until Jennifer, Sue's four-year-old, saw her mother carrying Mike, and let out a wail.

We decided to set a principle and said, "You all have to walk." We were only about a quarter of the way around the loop. *If* we were smart moms, we would have turned around then. Hindsight is 20/20 though.

Sue's four-year-old was afraid of the dog. When the dog got too close to the petite girl she looked so frightened that her mother had to pick her up to get past the beast.

Mike said once again, "I can't go any farther!" I picked him up. He's not very heavy and I felt sorry for him. But, as soon as my muscular 40 pound, son saw me carrying the neighbor boy he ran to me, clung to my legs and whimpered as if I didn't love him at all.

By now, we were at the half-way mark. We knew that going back would not be any shorter. We had to go on. Our delightful walk in the woods with the flora and fauna turned into a game like musical chairs, but instead it was called musical children. My little four-year-old friend, Amy, had me convinced that her body was not made for walking in the woods. Even my 10-year-old, Sarah, was carrying someone for part of the time. Sue and I would each carry a child until another child at our heels persuaded us to carry him or her.

The trail is rather pleasant, from an aesthetic point of view. There are wooden bridges, wild flowers, interesting stumps, vines, and berries. However most of the time my view was blocked by a sweaty youngster's smiling face. Sue and I had hoped to discuss mothering, life, the world--you know grown-up things. Instead, we talked about how much each child weighed and our feet kept tripping over a big wet dog.

The moral of the story?

If you are thinking about going for a one-mile-walk in the woods with a one-year-old, a two-year-old, two three-year-olds, one four-year-old, a six-year-old, an eight-year-old, and ten-year-old--plus--a big wet stray dog--*and* it's a sticky 80 degrees.

Stay home. Sit under a shade tree. Eat popsicles instead.

LESSON OF THE CICADA
SIMPLE, NATURAL

You can hear them zinging on hot summer days. Their high-pitched ringing can be loud enough to disturb your thoughts or just melodious enough to enhance your dreams.

I'd heard the sound long before I knew its origin. Someone mentioned "cicada" but I didn't know what they were.

One July day, a few years back, my friend Mary came to visit. She said, "Listen to the locusts. They sure are loud."

I said, "Just what exactly are locusts?"

Mary looked at me, quite shocked and said, "You don't know? You never collected their empty shells from trees?"

I was intrigued. "What do you mean? What do they look like?"

She explained the grasshopper-like insect to me. It crawls up from the ground and climbs trees. It sheds its skin by anchoring its feet onto rough tree bark, picnic tables, fences, etc. Through a thin crack in the back of its skin, it pulls its wet greenish body out of its brown see-through hard shell.

I said, "Hmm… think I'll look for one." I went to our box elder tree and scanned up and down. Suddenly, my eyes bulged and my pulse quickened as I looked at this strange, brown, hard-shelled insect on the tree.

Its eyes were also bulged and its delicate curved legs were firmly attached to the tree bark. It was motionless. So was I – never having seen such a thing. I quietly ran over to Mary and said, "Come here, I think I found a locust!"

Mary followed me and said, "Yup, you found one all right." Then, she gently tugged the little creature off the tree.

Being squeamish, I was interested but didn't want to get close. It was not actually a locust, just the shell of one. It had such a life-like body--head, eyes, legs, back, and abdomen--but it was empty!

I was baffled and intrigued. I didn't mind holding the little guy when I realized that he was not *really* there!

I showed my children how to hunt for shells. They found quite a collection. We even watched a few locusts as they shed their skin, at a glacial pace. Once they slid out of their shell, they remained on the tree to dry out their wings before flying away. My kids enjoyed showing their tree ornaments to unsuspecting company. Many visitors felt my initial leeriness.

In the fall of that year, I went to the wake of a woman I'd known for years. She was quite elderly and had died without suffering.

When I approached the casket to say a prayer for her and goodbye to this dear woman, I saw her lying there and could not help but think of the cicada. This body was a mere shell. The woman was not there. She had left. It all seemed so clear, simple, and natural.

THE SHADES AND SOUNDS OF LATE JULY

The foliage is ultra green this late July. The air is heavy; sky is a gray preview of a coming storm. We've received a lot of rain lately, though not enough to make the corn a bumper crop. But, that's what farming is all about: planting, wishing, hoping, waiting, and harvesting what you get.

Raspberry is another July color. Mauve, violet, and fuchsia stains appear on your hands when you're busy picking gems off hedgerows and creek bed bushes. But, your painted hands tell only part of the story. The anticipation of finding ripe fruit begging to be a pie, that cozy feeling of flannel sleeves protecting your arms, feeling your jeans soak up moisture from the pressing vegetation, all make picking berries a rich experience. The deep, repetitive thud of berries landing in your plastic bucket changes to a muted bump as the bottom of your pail is covered.

What's big, fat, striped green on the outside and luscious red with dark brown seeds on the inside? It's family reunion time, where love is shared and passed around like watermelon on paper plates. Family reunions are quite theatrical. Unfortunately, there are no dress rehearsals.

People arrive hoping for harmony. Often times, however, personalities clash like cymbals. People pipe in with advice. Some harp on others' shortcomings, while kids are always chiming in. But you know what? You can't expect a perfect symphony at annual gatherings. You have to keep on loving the musicians, even those who are tone deaf.

One day at our reunion, numerous family members climbed Owl's Head Mountain. The many shades of green on the trail were almost too much for our eyes to digest. We saw crystal clear water trickling down a cliff and found a slate black cave we imagined was a home for black bears. We entered the cave like Goldilocks, our hearts pounding. My children, sisters, brothers-in-law, nieces, and nephews were armed with flashlights, courage, fright and excitement. We explored the hard rock interior and found one tiny spider, a puddle of water, and some sticks. Being in such an unusual setting was thrilling. Our joyous voices echoed harmoniously in exploration.

Back at the farm, green frogs with their rubbery yellow bellies croak and boast in the pond, happy with the recent rains.

And a blue, red, yellow, striped and polka-dotted ball goes sailing through the air as the kids' scream and continue their kickball game.

Hot air balloons with colorful designs dot the July evening skies, moving with majestic grace, like jewels hanging in the air.

Late July with its long--eared days and drawn--out nights, holds all kinds of shades and sounds.

HIDE A LITTLE TOY
IN MASHED POTATOES

The toy in a cereal box can have tremendous power over a young boy. My six-year-old son Scotty loves cereal. He doesn't necessarily want cereal for breakfast; often he has waffles or bagels. He wants cereal for dinner, like when I've fixed a big roast beef or chicken meal. Scotty figures that cereal is quick and delicious. Sometimes there's even a surprise at the bottom of the box!

(Maybe I should hide whistles in the mashed potatoes…)

If there is a toy in the cereal, he will go to great lengths to get it. The other day, I got home from grocery shopping around 10:30 a.m. While I was putting away the contents of 12 bags of groceries, my son, who was munching on an apple, started telling me how hungry he was. I said, "We'll eat lunch soon. Wait until I get these groceries put away." He looked at me like a stray pup and whined,

"But I'm starving!" While I continued putting the food away, he moaned as if he was at his last gasp. Finally, I said, "OK, you can eat lunch now, but not cereal!" Hoping to include more food groups, I said, "Have a sandwich."

We compromised. He had half a ham/cheese/lettuce sandwich, followed by a big bowl of Rice Krispies. While he was eating his beloved cereal, he noticed the new box of Rice Krispies that I was about to put away and asked to look at it.

Scotty instantly noticed that there was a glow-in-the-dark, talking, skeleton head inside the unopened box. His brain computed the necessary steps--according to the rules of our house. He must finish the old box to open the new.

He quickened his munching and yelled, "More cereal please!"

I said, "Are you sure?"

And he replied, "Yes, I'm really starving."

Now, lucky for my six-year-old, he has a younger brother who thinks that anything that the older brother does is cool. So Johnny said, "I want what Scotty's having!"

I poured a second bowl for Scott and then a bowl for Johnny. Scott worked fast and said, "More please!"

I replied, "No, that's enough, you'll get a stomach ache."

But he insisted, "No I won't. I'm really hungry!" A bit reluctantly I poured a third bowl for the aspiring magician. As I poured it, I went easy with the serving but Scotty could almost see the bottom of the old box and pleaded, "Ah c'mon, Mom, give me more."

I gave him half a bowl and said, "Listen pal, if you finish this and still want more then you can have more."

He thrust his spoon into the bowl and continued his mission. Part way through bowl number three, Scotty let out a groan. I asked, "Are you OK?"

He said, "Yeah," and almost resumed eating, but his eyes crossed as he looked at the wall to center himself.

I said, "You don't have to eat anymore. I think you are full."

Scott replied, "I'm sorry," got down from his chair and went into the other room.

Later that afternoon I told my husband about Scott's gallant attempt to get the coveted prize. Being a sweet dad, Greg said, "Ah, get the magic trick out for him."

And I did.

FARMING IS FAMILY FUN

Johnny and I rode on the tractor with Greg while he baled wheat straw. Our three-year-old Johnny likes tractors more than ice cream, candy, gum or TV. I love his excitement as he climbs aboard a tractor. We got settled under the open cab of the John Deere and rode out toward the wheat field. The sky was soft blue with wispy white clouds. The sun was hot, the air dry. Cicadas were screaming but a slight wind carried their music away.

We reached a crossroad on the farm where four different crops meet. The oats were tan in color and nearly ready to harvest. The corn beyond the oats was tasseled out and in pretty good shape considering our dry June. The alfalfa field was a rich dark green with lavender purple blossoms on each plant. The smell of the flowers was so sweet. I closed my eyes to inhale the fragrance without distraction. The wheat field on the fourth corner was a capturing design. Greg had combined the wheat earlier and now was about to bale up the long rows of golden straw.

The whine of the tractor and, grinding click of the baler were surprisingly soothing. Watching the baler was enlightening and fun. It moves automatically, pulling up straw, twirling it into the baler compartment and throws rectangular--shaped bales back to land in the wagon. It gives me goose bumps to know that man has invented such a complex machine to produce colorful, fragrant, bales. Afterward, seeing the graphic lines in the field from the hilltop is awe-inspiring.

The three-sided wagon with its gray weathered wood had the appearance of soft flannel, pleasing gray with flowing white shadows. It is interesting how hardwood can suggest cloth-like softness.

Johnny was in his glory. He sat motionless and totally absorbed in the operation. That boy has "farming" written all over his face. Everything on the farm interests him.

Queen Anne's lace dotted the hedges. It was fun imagining ladybugs meeting at the flowers' edges. I could picture them pulling up leaves to sit on and leaning on the crocheted tablecloths, discussing their families.

Butterflies performed like ballerinas all around the wheat field.

After a couple of rounds, Johnny and I caught a ride home with Pop, who was bringing empty wagons out to Greg.

Lucky Greg stayed out there baling up the rest of the straw. He could continue to smell the sweet alfalfa, watch the butterfly ballets, and eavesdrop on ladybugs, while I fixed supper.

P.S. In all fairness, baling straw is more involved than that. While Johnny and I got to ride and enjoy the view, Greg had to listen to the clicks and grinds to make sure there wasn't a malfunctioning clunk. He had to look ahead to stay in the row and look behind him to make sure that the bales were landing in the wagon. He perhaps does not see the imaginary ladybugs at their tea-party and can only watch an occasional curtsey from a butterfly. However, he can certainly smell the alfalfa blossoms. The aroma permeates you, and lifts you right out of your seat.

MINNOW 'STING' OPERATION A SUCCESS

Tonight we went minnow-ing! Greg decided that one person should wear boots. Somehow I got volunteered. Greg drove the pickup. The four children, three nets, one large plastic pail and I piled into the back of the truck. We jostled across the fields to the creek.

We searched for a good minnow spot and found a decent one. Greg said that we needed a *thinner* channel, though, so we bush-whacked through the brush to another perfectly fine area. But Greg announced loudly, "Naw. Turn back, this won't do!" So we all turned around, filed back to the truck and moved on down the creek.

We examined a third bend in the raging current (actually just a trickling creek) and Greg said, "Nope. Let's look farther down."

We all swarmed back to the idling vehicle. This time I figured I'd walk to commune with the birds and wild flowers.

I hummed along until something seemed to drive a 10-penny nail into the front of my ankle. "Wow!" I yelled jumping, and furiously trying to wrench my rubber boot off. As the yellow wading boot went flying, a huge creature flew with it. I don't know what stung me, but my ankle swelled and throbbed.

We went behind our neighbor's house where minnows were recently sighted.

Greg was in charge of the capture. My orders were to find a big stick, walk up stream and make a splashing racket while wading toward him. He stood with a foot on each bank, the possibly man-eating minnows darting through the water between his feet. The creek is about four inches deep and about 1 ½ feet wide. Greg positioned all three nets in precise formation so that no minnow could get by his fool-proof trap. The kids stood on the bank, holding a pail of creek water, ready to fill it up with tons of tiny fish.

I thrashed the forked stick back and forth through the water. Minnows scooted in every direction. When I met Greg at his post, he proudly lifted his strategically placed nets out of the water. Not one teeny, tiny fish!

I said, "Great plan, Greg," then proceeded to take a net from him. Laura took another one. She and I lowered the nets into the water, swished them around, and each came up with four or five wiggling trophies.

Eventually, we got quite a few from haphazard luck. We finished up with about an ounce of fish, one very sore ankle and four pretty muddy kids.

Greg and the children walked over the pond to empty the pail of our prize catch. I sat in a lawn chair with my foot elevated on another chair. My ankle throbbed but I was happy. I was eating an ice cream cone and our sting operation was a success. Sort of.

YAY! JOHNNY'S NOT A BABY ANYMORE

Or Ravishing Rick Rude Cleaned My Kitchen Today...

Our three-year-old son Johnny has just graduated from babyhood and I am ecstatic. So many times I hear the advisors in my life say, "Appreciate your children when they're young. They grow up so fast. Don't rush them. When they're little there are little problems; when they get bigger so do the problems."

Hold it. I love babies. I adore them. All babies melt my heart in one second. I love their little features: their wondering, curious eyes', miniature fingers', gummy smiles, and sweet, sweet slumber.

But let me tell you. Now that my youngest is out of diapers, sleeps in a big bed, climbs in and out of the bath tub, can tiptoe to wash his hands on the sink, will sit quietly for a whole story, can tell me what hurts and why, can be trusted alone outside for almost a minute, is learning to share his toys with youngsters, can do the doggy paddle in the water, and will stay downstairs without a locked gate preventing him from running upstairs and getting into toothpaste, hand cream, makeup, or his brother's remote control car, this is an exciting time worth sharing.

Why did so many people try to convince me that the work would never ease up, that the burden would get bigger and heavier? Well…perhaps because…Yesterday morning at around 8:30, I came into the house after unloading two wagons of hay. My two girls eight and 10 met me at the door with dazzling smiles. They had taken baths, washed their hair, eaten breakfast and swept the floors. Sarah was about to wash dishes, and Laura was dusting. Scott had made his and Johnny's beds, and picked up all of the toys.

I just about needed smelling salts. The children did all of this on their own. I was jolted back to reality when the assembled looked at me with pleading eyes and scrubbed faces. And together they said, "Mom, now that we did *all* of this work, *oh* and we're going to clean the bathroom too, can we please watch pro-wrestling today?"

Maybe *this* is what other people are trying to tell me. Children learn how to outsmart parents. I despise wrestling. I find it dumb, repulsive even. I think it encourages aggressive behavior. It's an enormous waste of time. I told the children a couple of weeks ago, "No more wrestling."

Now folks, what would you have done in my shoes? I looked around at the clean house and at their sweet; eager faces and said, "OK. Just for today."

They won that match.

Then, during dinner, I had to hear about Hulk Hogan and Macho Man becoming a fierce pair, about Andre the Giant team-ing up with the Million Dollar Man, and the horrible details about Ravishing Rick Rude trying to kiss Jake the Snake's wife. Gross.

Maybe I should clean the house before unloading the hay.

A PERFECT NIGHT FOR A HAYRIDE

After supper, the kids and I went for a walk up the road. We thought that we could catch a ride on a wagon full of hay. Greg was baling up two wagons of second cut. When we got to the field, he was nearly finished.

Walking through the clean hayfield was fun. Every time we took a step, grasshoppers hopped out of our path. With five of us walking, so many grasshoppers made the field effervescent, as though we were walking on bubbly ginger ale.

The air was cool—you could feel summer giving way to fall. It's as though fall stopped by to make reservations. The nights are downright nippy and the colors all around are changing. The moon was about half full, bright and dominant in the dark blue sky.

We all tried to catch grasshoppers while Greg baled up the last row of raked hay. Sarah caught a grasshopper and put it on my finger. I enjoyed studying its shape and color. My little pet seemed quite content to perch on my finger until Laura held her grasshopper right next to mine. *Boing!* My friend sprang away.

In the meantime, neighbors ambled out of their houses and walked over the hayfield. Supper time was over and there's nothing like a family walk outside on a cleaned hay field with grasshoppers boinging, the moon shining, and crickets chirping.

Little red-haired Ryan ran across the field, his diaper impervious to hay stubble. Patsy was smiling as her son Nick waved from the tractor. (Nick was already up on the fender of Greg's tractor.) Big Rick ran with his dog Bear galloping after him. Debbie and Dorothy visited while Amy, Mike, Sean and Chris ran around, their energy free and happy.

When Greg finished baling, we all decided, instantly to ride the wagon back to the farm. Sue, Jennifer and Danielle ran over to join us. Climbing into the pile of rectangular stacks was fun. We passed babies up and over the wooden rail. We started to resemble the grasshoppers on the ground. When each of us had found our perfect seat, Greg pulled us around the field and even through a hedge.

What a thrill--a spontaneous hayride! The moon followed us as we sailed down the road, singing and laughing. One of us (I won't mention Dorothy's name) got lodged between bales and began to sink, legs going in different directions and her derriere getting lost in the shuffle. We laughed like children. I imagined we looked like flowers in a rock garden.

It's interesting how an innocent stroll on a quiet evening turned into a hootenanny. That's the charm of living in the country!

FAIR PLACE TO SHOWCASE NEW YORK'S FINEST

Before going to the State Fair, my children wanted to know what to expect. The word "Fair" to them meant rides, lots of rides. I explained that, yes, there would be rides, but much more than that. There would be exhibits of New York's finest cows, sleekest horses, and prize-winning pigs. Others would bring in healthy vegetables, hand-made clothes, and well groomed bunnies. I said, "There's so much to see at the Fair."

We stood in line at the parking garage with a lot of early risers. A group of people appeared to be developmentally disabled. They wore official identification cards pinned to their clothes and proudly informed us that they needed to arrive early to clean the bathrooms.

The ride to the fair was fun. Our bus was clean, air conditioned, with comfortable seats. We looked out the big side windows and, being up so high, we were able to get a great perspective of the countryside.

We went to the poultry building and saw many varieties of chickens, roosters, and geese. Some were unusually small and others amazingly big. Some had red bumps all over their faces, while others had feathers down their legs and even on their feet. We saw rabbits of every size, shape, and color. In the middle of the room was a big glassed-in area that held swans and other graceful water fowl. Also enjoying the fine array of beautiful birds was a man strapped to a stretcher, accompanied by a caregiver.

We went into the Energy Building. There were so many people in there at the same time that getting around was a bit difficult. I'm sure that the lady with the face mask, in the wheelchair, felt the congestion in the room.

There was so much to see and do. Shows were scheduled throughout the day. We saw a dog show and a seatbelt demonstration showing how important it is to buckle-up. The demonstration volunteer traveled at only 5 mph. When he struck a cushioned barrier, his body violently jolted forward.

Energetic young boys and girls participated in a talent show. They sang and danced (tap, jazz, modern) and played instruments. I saw a man pushing a pretty young woman in a wheelchair appreciating the agile dancers.

We thoroughly enjoyed a high dive performance. Olympic divers dove and clowned around from very high altitudes. One of the one-foot square platforms was 70 to 80 feet high. The divers were precise and their bodies were in great shape. I noticed an elderly woman in a wheelchair behind me enjoying these demonstrations of skill.

We watched another act in which skiers soared down a bristle ramp, flipped through the air, then landed in a standing position on a large, rubber mattress. Simultaneously, men bounced on trampolines and accomplished acrobatic feats in the air. An elderly man in a wheelchair sat near me.

We enjoyed seeing our favorite newscasters from the local TV station being filmed directly the fairgrounds.

We ate delicious baked potatoes, held newborn chicks and ducklings, went on a few rides, tried to win goldfish, and saw many different kinds of game fish that live in New York's waters, and a big stuffed black bear and a real soft, long haired llama.

Through the buildings and along the midway we saw a variety of exhibits and people. But the lasting impression I have from the fair is the number of people of all ages who were in wheelchairs or walked or talked with apparent difficulty. When I think of the daily challenges that these people endure and overcome, I'm embarrassed at my daily complaints. And I'm so glad that the fair is accessible to everyone.

Yes indeed, the Fair is an exhibition of our States finest!

CLOUDY, SPARKY MEET FISHER PRICE

Sarah and Laura, our 10 and eight-year-old daughters have wanted a pet ever since our cinnamon-colored, house cat, Jason, died last year.

A few months ago, we got some chickens. We soon realized it is difficult to play with chickens. They are only fluffy and cuddly for a few weeks. And quite frankly, now that they are full grown, they are a bit frightening. Their beaks are long and sharp. Their heads dart nervously.

When the roosters flap their wings they appear large and menacing to frighten predators and discourage rival roosters. Hearing them learn to crow has been fun. It started as a "cock-a," became a "cock-a-doodle," and finally graduated to a fully fledged "cock-a-doodle-doo!" What a great early morning sound.

The hens should start laying eggs in October. Collecting the eggs will be an adventure.

The girls wanted a pet they could hold and cuddle. The droves of barn cats and kittens were not sufficient because they don't come into the house.

For three days, every time I turned my head, there was a young girl looking at me with gerbil eyes saying, "Please!"

Being a conscientious and decisive mother, I passed the buck and said, "It's up to your father."

Greg can tease unmercifully and for one whole day he had the girls walking on eggshells. "Gerbil Talks" became as meaningful as "Summit Talks". Deals, promises, pledges, clauses, all had to be worked out. Finally, after day three of bargaining, Greg said, "I don't care. It's really up to your mom."

Do other parents behave this way?

Day three of negotiations, we sealed the pact. With their own money, the girls purchased two furry little guys; tan and white Cloudy, black and white Sparky, two lbs. of appetizing gerbil food, and three lbs. of aromatic wood shavings.

Fortunately for the girls, their sweet Aunt Linda is letting them use her old gerbil home.

Even though the creatures resemble mice, I prefer to look at them as tiny rabbits with long skinny tails. Cloudy and Sparky are actually quite cute and have managed to make us all smile.

The other day, Sarah and Laura set up a giant maze on the floor. It seemed funny to see the old Fisher Price castle come alive with little gerbils running around the drawbridge. They peeked out over the castle tower and ran down the interior to a window. Their little faces peered out the window, whiskers twitching, and then they jumped onto a waiting Tonka dump-truck.

Next, they ran across the xylophone and under the Playskool airplane. I wonder if these major toy companies have ever imagined that their creative toys would be used to stimulate gerbils!

Pets make a house a home. They quickly become an integral part of the family. But they are work and have unique needs and demands. So far, Cloudy and Sparky are quite content gnawing on discarded toilet paper rolls.

This morning, as the girls left for their first day of school, they gave me my orders. (I do not remember this in the contract.) "Mom, every now and then check on Cloudy and Sparky. If they look bored, give them a paper cup to chew on."

What does a bored gerbil look like?

FROM MY JOURNAL, SEPT. 13, 1988:

I've kept a journal for many years. As a matter of fact, I have about 10 notebooks filled. Unlike writing a diary it's more about what I'm thinking and feeling than a record of what I did each day and includes prayers, questions, even some artwork.

Writing in my journal is like time spent with a friend. I don't worry about what I say or how I say it. I just open up and let the words topple on the paper ignoring correct grammar or proper editing. It's a bit crude, but honest. Above all, honest.

It's difficult coming up with 500 worthwhile words for a newspaper column every week. I hear mixed reactions from people. I've received numerous compliments but people have different likes and dislikes. Some people love it when I write about farm life. Others like to read about the children's adventures. And others haven't told me anything, leaving me wondering.

You know, Lord, I need Your help with this column. It was Your and my shared responsibility right from the start. Please give a clue what I should do. If You want me to back off from this weekly challenge, please let me know. It's quite draining. Feels like I'm pulling out part of me when I write some of these. This journalizing isn't tiring or difficult. On the contrary, it's enjoyable and therapeutic.

Kids are doing well in school. We are pleased with Owasco School. Things seem to be settled down now. The first few days were a bit jumbled.

The *winter* wheat is in the ground and it soaked up today's rainfall. Interesting how it's planted in late summer then harvested the following mid-summer, instead of typical spring planting and fall harvesting.

Hmm…I just got a brave notion to use today's journal as next week's column.

Just knowing that I might use this in the paper takes away that free-flowing feeling. I'm starting to struggle with this now.

A column, takes more discipline. I can't ramble on about my feelings. I need to keep things neat and tidy so that I won't appear to be a *neurotic* mother, wife, home engineer, farmer, baby-sitter, gardener, nurse, launderer, accountant, vegetable and fruit freezer, writer, etc.

When I asked The Citizen if I could write a weekly column, I was bursting with ideas. Now, after six months and 24 columns, my fire is under control and sometimes, like today, it wanes.

Well, I feel better. I'm going to count how many words I've written and if it's close to 500 I just might be brave enough to type it up and hand it in. But I doubt if I'm that bold.

By the way, there are 449 words.

WEAVING FRIENDSHIPS AND WREATHS

My nose felt like a factory that was working around the clock, with all of its turbines in full gear. Sometimes circuit breakers would shut off and breathing through my nostrils would be history. Just an old head cold, but it had me down in the dumps.

Then, I got two phone calls from friendly neighbors, Debbie and Sue. They were coming down with their kids and we were going out to walk in the sunshine. Big doses of vitamin D sounded like a good idea.

The morning turned out to be so much fun that I plumb forgot about my stuffed-up head.

Before we went outside, the girls were discussing grapevine wreaths. Sue casually mentioned that Debbie had started to show her how to make one. I got upset and said, "Why couldn't you show me, too? You said you would!"

Debbie said, "Keep your pants on, for Pete's sake, I'll show you right now!" (This is how we talk to each other.)

We all headed across the street for the pond. Johnny and Mike rode the tractor with Greg who was going to pull out more of the hedge with the backhoe.

We walked along the field as Debbie assured us how easy it would be to make some wreaths. I was skeptical. First of all, the only wild grapes that I knew of were the ones behind our house, not across the street. And I'd been told that to make wreaths you must pick them during the proper season and soak them for hours in some special mixture to make them pliable. I always thought that it would take careful planning and designated timing.

We got to the pond in a hurry. We followed Debbie as she marched over to the hedge. After a quick scan of the foliage, she pulled and yanked and grunted, then yelled, "Aren't you going to help?" So, Sue and I gave her some assistance and together we freed a long wild grape vine. (I soon realized that I'd seen those vines growing all over the farm, in different hedges.)

Debbie began pulling off leaves and quicker than instant oatmeal, created a giant wreath, just by winding it up like a garden hose. We pulled out greener, more flexible vines, wrapped them around, tucked them in, and TA DA!

We were totally absorbed. We each made two wreaths in less than an hour. The youngsters ran up on the hayfield. Their backdrop was the giant blue fall sky with white swirls of clouds. According to the calendar it was still summer, but we knew it was a fall day. The colored leaves floating on the surface of the pond, the chill in the air that made us wear sweaters and sweatshirts, and the purple grapes that clung to their vines, all told us that fall had unpacked his bags and was making himself comfortable.

While Greg was pulling out brush, he snagged a big clump of vines with the backhoe and dumped them at our feet. We whirled and twirled, bent and twisted the tenuous wood. It was easy to do and very therapeutic. I felt like an Indian maiden which gave me great pleasure. I so admire the skills and closeness that Native Americans have with nature.

Now, all that we have to do is pick some dried fall weeds to add to our wreaths, and maybe add a satin ribbon or a bit of lace, and they'll be as pretty as ever. Or, we could just leave them plain; they are quite beautiful. The delicate curls of the vines are so inspiring. They seem able to accept any path, any obstacle. They simply adapt by curling around neighboring branches and cling to each other for support and strength.

Wreaths are like friendships—an intermingling of talents and time spent together, weaving in laughter with shared problems. (There were some thorny bushes in the hedges.) A single strand will not make a wreath, but many strands combine for a strong bond.

P.S. My prescription for anyone with a cold on a sunny fall day? Find yourself a friend or two, some wild vines, and weave a memory.

FROST CONTRIBUTES TO BEAUTY OF FALL

I believe that every day holds new promise. Today promised to start out quite dramatically. The black barn roof was white. The grass and vegetable garden were shrouded in frost. We didn't cover our tomatoes and flowerbeds last night. Around 6:15 a.m., Greg sprayed cold water on the plants to keep them from dying. This first frost will have a big effect on the crops and landscape. Corn will start to dry faster and farmers can think about combining their corn. Leaves will change color more rapidly now.

Isn't it great when you see a tree that is such a beautiful color, you are moved to take in a deep breath to meditate briefly on the wonder of nature?

Yesterday was just another day. My friend Debbie and I decided to drive to Empire Cheese in Skaneateles Junction to buy some of their great cheddar. My father-in-law, Pop, came with us for the ride. Johnny and I climbed into the back seat with Debbie's children, Amy and Mikey. We all looked forward to the mini-excursion. On the way, I had told them all about the many animals we'd be able to see at a big farm on our way there. However, when we drove by the farm where peacocks used to run out to greet us, and geese, ducks and chickens usually strutted by the road, we saw very few birds, maybe because of the cooler temperatures.

We drove down through a cloud of dust down a road that was recently oiled and listened as tiny stones bounced off Debbie's car. Naturally she had just washed and waxed. The three children, Deb and I went inside the plant and were disappointed to learn there the cheese wouldn't be available until November 1 due to the office relocating to another part of the building.

Back in the Jeep, Johnny cried because he couldn't sit by the window. Our fun excursion was going a little haywire. Fortunately the colors of the countryside took our minds from our worries and lifted our spirits. The fields of golden rod and purple aster, red and orange trees, and flocks of geese honking and waving enriched the day.

Just as we walked in the door of our home, the phone rang. Harriet Smith Marshall, an 89-year-old woman, had recently read my story about the grapevine wreaths. She wanted to know if I could make some small ones for her granddaughters.

The six of us traipsed outside again, walking behind the barn, through the pumpkin patch, over the top of the plow, and through the weeds. Debbie and I began to pull out some grapevines. Meanwhile, Amy got burdocks in her hair and started to cry. Pop tried to pull the burdocks out while Debbie and I tugged at vines and Johnny and Mike played hide and seek in the tall weeds.

Maybe you had to be there to understand the spontaneous charms of this fall day.

Three-year-old Johnny took a good nap, and I enjoyed winding vines to decorate the home of Harriet's grandchildren.

The space shuttle is scheduled to come down today. This could be more than just another day.

LIFE'S SEASONS: A PRISM FROM PATSY

Fall is displaying its abilities in crimson and gold outside my big kitchen window this morning. I'm not sure what our friend, Patsy McGinnis, can see from her hospital bed. Hopefully, she is near a window and can view multi-colored leaves spread out on dark green grass or a bed of bold yellow and gold marigolds.

Patsy is back in the hospital in Boston. She had a liver transplant last fall. For a while she was doing great, then suffered a rejection and had to go back to the hospital for an extended stay. When she returned home, she remained weak, but still managed to help her son Nick achieve his Boy Scout badges. Patsy swam at the YMCA to get therapeutic exercise. She took a course to become a hospice volunteer. She went on a camping retreat to rejuvenate her spirit and ever-deepening faith. Just recently she baked and decorated a clown cake for her son's birthday. The cake was so adorable that I felt guilty eating its big smile.

The day after Nicholas's birthday, Patsy's name went on the list for people waiting for a new liver. The liver that she received last year did the best it could, but now her body demands another liver that is more compatible. However, she's taking antibiotics intravenously for two to three weeks because of a fungus infection that developed on her ankle. She cannot get a transplant while receiving antibiotics for the infection on her ankle.

Due to her weakened condition for so many months, Patsy's legs gave out and she hurt her back. The doctors are trying to determine exactly what is causing her back pain so that she can walk. Right now, she barely shuffles around with a walker.

I was with my children before they got on the bus this morning. But Patsy has not seen her son Nicholas for two weeks.

I must confess that Patsy does have one fault. She does not complain. It drives me crazy. You know how it is when you get with a friend, you share your problems, take turns listening and complaining and you both feel better. Well, Patsy is an excellent listener but she's a terrible complainer. I always feel better after we visit because she radiates hope. She and God seem to have a pretty strong connection. Patsy knew one day that I was feeling low and disappointed with all of the pits in life's cherries. She sent a beautifully wrapped package to me. Inside a little box was a prism with these instructions:

Bobbie,

Read the story of Noah and the Ark, Genesis 6:5-9:17. Put the prism in your window. When you see a rainbow on the floor wall, etc., remember God is with you always even when you are depressed and hurting and lonely. He doesn't want you to hurt. He is always there to draw strength from. Don't fight him let him help you.

Peace and Love
Patsy

Patsy's faith has been a constant well for me to draw from. Whenever I see rainbows on the kitchen chairs or the side of the refrigerator, I smile.

At Nicholas's recent birthday party, while we gobbled up the clown, Patsy mentioned how she loves hearing from people while she's in the hospital. Letters, cards, and notes really do cheer her up. She said that she likes hearing about daily events as simple as they are. I told you she's a good listener.

…Pasty, a school nurse in the Auburn School District passed away on April 1, 1995…

TOUGH MOMS DON'T FAINT
WHEN KID'S SICK

10-year-old Sarah came downstairs yesterday morning, complaining of a sore throat. I listened to her complaint, and then advised her to eat breakfast. I try not to give too much attention to early morning woes. It can be difficult to decide when a child should stay home, and when they are well enough to go to school. Sometimes, the symptoms of an illness are loud and clear. Other times the child appears fine. If I search my memory, I can recall a few times that I stayed home from school pretending to be sick. One time, I burrowed way down under the covers of my bed and stayed there until I felt real warm. Then, I went into my mother's room and said, "Mom, I feel warm. I must have a fever." Unfortunately, the walk through the halls of our big old house cooled me down by the time I got to Mom's room.

Sarah ate a few bits of oatmeal, and then complained of a headache. I felt her brow and said, "You feel fine, Sarah. No fever."

Then, when she said, "My stomach kind of hurts too!" I began to get curious. Ah ha! I remembered what the school day had in store for her.

I said, "Are you sure it's not your three tests today that bother you? Thinking that I'd done my detective work, I added, "I think you'll be fine. You're ready for your tests. Don't be nervous."

Sarah sat with a questioning look on her face. I attributed it to her wondering how her Mom could be so smart to figure out the real problem. In retrospect, she was probably trying to figure out what her tests had to do with how crummy she felt.

Sarah came home from school with a loaded book bag and a pale face. She slumped in a chair and said, "I feel terrible." I felt her head and said, "Oh, you poor girl! You sure have a fever now!" Guilty thoughts skittered through my mind. I should have listened to her. I gave her some Tylenol, sat her by the wood-burning stove and apologized for not tuning in better.

I had to work at the polls for registration after supper. When I came home at 9:15 p.m., the children were tucked in their beds, their Dad had helped them with their homework, and when I asked him how Sarah's evening was, he said, "Good! She did her homework, ate supper and seemed pretty well."

However, the next time I saw Sarah, she was not well. At 1:30 a.m., she was standing next to my bed, whispering. I reached my hand out of the covers and felt her forehead. It was hot. I said, "C'mon, Sarah, let's go to the bathroom for some Tylenol."

I don't know about the rest of the world, but if I get out of bed too quickly I get real dizzy, maybe due to low blood sugar. Well, since I was still carrying guilt from the afternoon and wanted to attend to Sarah as soon as possible, I hurriedly reached up to get the bottle of pills on the top shelf of the closet. My head started to spin as I said, "Ut oh!" I knew that my legs were going to give way and I would drop to the floor. Everything inside my eyes began to get dark. I controlled my fall to the cold bathroom linoleum floor and said weakly, "I'll help you in a minute, Sarah."

Once again I saw a quizzical look on Sarah's face that almost said, "You're a real big help, Mom."

Sarah slumped to her knees and put her head on the chair. We looked at each other under the bright clinical bathroom light, and half-smiled. We looked like a couple of loony-tunes.

After a few minutes, I pulled myself up, wrestled with the childproof cap, handed Sarah a capsule, and everything started to go black again. Oh, for Pete's sake! I hit the deck as gently as I could.

Sarah put the bottle high up on the shelf. Watching her move around the bathroom, helping me help her, was strange.

But by the next morning, we laughed about it. I think that the memory will be etched in our minds forever. Sarah didn't go to school today. I'm not the least bit dizzy (some might debate that). Now, I can wait on her with ease.

My husband, Greg, said that I should have called to him to come help us. Why didn't I think of that?

It's important to take care of your sick children. Of course it really helps not to faint while doing so.

AN EGGS-OTIC DAY

Yesterday my husband came in from the barn after doing chores. In his hand, he held a small, smooth, brown, oblong egg that amazed us with its perfection of form.

We've had our chickens for six months. We were told to expect eggs in six months. Hooray! It finally happened.

It's funny how much excitement was created from the smooth little object. While the kids were dressing for school, I ran around the house, showing it to each of them. Squeals of delight mixed with cries of "Can I hold it?"

Now for the dilemma; we're a family of seven, counting Pop. Who gets to eat the prized poultry product? Should I poach it, scramble it, or make a mini-omelet? Perhaps we could have it bronzed. Better yet, we could blow out the inside and decorate it for Easter.

In the midst of everyone passing it back and forth, it got dropped, went splat and ended our dilemma.

After the egg incident, I went to Auburn Memorial Hospital for my employment orientation. I'm going to start work there, two days a week, as a Radiologic Technologist. I worked there twelve years and four children ago. The hospital has changed dramatically. There's been so much renovation, additions, beautiful paintings and art work added. Soft two-tone shades of beige and blue replace the louder colors.

My column might take on a new angle. It might be X-RAY/TED.

Back home after lunch and the children's nap, Amy, the little girl who I take care of came into the kitchen holding her bloody mouth. She was crying and sputtering and finally managed to tell me that Johnny, my sweet, adorable, three-year-old, kicked out her tooth.

At face value it sounds terrible, right? But when we got the blood washed off Amy's mouth and found the tooth on the living room floor the story was put into perspective.

Amy and Johnny were playing and Amy was sort of kicking Johnny and he sort of kicked her back (fortunately, he only had socks on). Her baby tooth had been loose for days. The real reason Amy was crying when her tooth went flying? She didn't think that we could find her tooth to put under her pillow.

From a little brown egg, to a sprawling hospital, to a kicked-out tooth, the day was interesting. How was your day?

WHEN THE GOING GETS TOUGH, READ A GOOD BOOK.

My aunt, Rita, died this week. She was a neat lady: tall, stately, charming and feisty. She had a long healthy life but her death still causes grief. Now that she has passed, our family is reminded of how temporary our time is here.

I don't feel encouraged about life right now.

It's raining fiercely. The wind thrashes water in every direction. Autumn leaves that clung to trees drop from the weight of the rain. It's hard to appreciate the beauty outside when the windows are covered with long, wavy rivulets as if the whole world is sharing my grief.

Death is hard to accept. It's as certain as a sun set though not as beautiful.

November is the time of cold rain, mud and dreary days. I get cabin fever when it gets dark early. We have to constantly load the wood burning stove to keep the house warm. Winter jackets hog the coat rack. Boots, hats, scarves and mittens are scattered about, looking for a comfortable spot.

Of course, it could have been much worse. I saw on the 6 o'clock news that Northern New York, where I'm from, is buried in about 14 inches of snow and slush. About 10,000 people have been without power for days. And here I was lamenting about the rain today.

This week has been one of acceptance. My husband, Greg, combined corn this week. The corn harvest is considerably less on account of the summer's drought.

Reading is a great way to enjoy a dreary day. Twice today I witnessed young children enjoying reading. At "Story Hour" at Seymour library, I watched the faces of three and four-year-olds fill with wonder as they eagerly listened to Mrs. Needham read to them. It's so easy to be transported to other lands, climates, situations, and conversations in books.

Later on I sat with our six-year-old son Scott and listened while he read his homework. He sounded out each letter and struggled at times, but his pride and enthusiasm were so apparent.

Reading can be a great escape or a great excursion. The Bible is an interesting book. I like to open it randomly to see what it has to say. It can be encouraging, filled with adventure, sibling relationships, infidelity, war, peace, jealousy, loaded with human behavior which hasn't changed all that much, even though these stories are thousands of years old. Guess the moral to today's column could be: "When the going gets tough, read a good book."

WILD ANIMALS GROUND ME

Whenever I see an animal in the wild, I feel excited. Driving along country roads, I enjoy the scenery. I love seeing hills, knolls, swamps and meadows. Domestic animals are interesting, but it's the bunny, chipmunk, deer or woodchuck—the surprise that lives in the wild that makes me smile.

This summer, my husband spotted a red fox in the plowed corn field. I got out the binoculars and watched the graceful animal as he ambled up the field. A few weeks later, the children and I were at the pond and saw something lying half-way up the young corn plants.

We walked slowly toward the sleeping animal. When we got within about 300 feet, a red fox looked up. It stared at us a while, and then slowly walked along the corn rows. We followed it, staying a safe distance behind. Eventually, it ran through the hedge and out of view. We were ecstatic to have seen such a gorgeous creature.

This past Sunday, my family and I took a drive to Waterloo. It rained torrentially most of the trip. We had fun visiting relatives and appreciated the safe journey. However, I was slightly disappointed when we got home. We hadn't seen any animals in the wild.

We did see a couple of loose calves. They were grazing by the side of the road. A farmer was heading toward them with his tractor. I hoped he had them rounded up and fenced-in quickly. We've had our share of loose cows—and it's usually when it's raining and the electric fence trips off.

We did pass a dead skunk in the road. Holy Toledo, I'd rather drive by a live skunk. The aroma of that guy stayed with us for many miles.

During our ride, we scanned the roadside but, alas, critters were probably in a sheltered place, out of the rain.

Today, however, I was rewarded, reimbursed or just lucky. Johnny and I ran lots of errands. We went to the carwash, bakery, and pet store, can redemption, department store, and then took the back way home.

We saw a buck. He was across the road on a hilly pasture standing at the top and looking around. As he turned, his points were visible like spread palms.

I pulled the car over and Johnny and I were mesmerized as the deer looked at us. The feeling inside of me was pure joy. My heart said, "Hey big guy. How are you? Are you getting enough food? Are you nervous about the pending doom of hunting season? Can you remain wild and free, healthy and at peace?"

The stately animal turned toward the fence, jumped over it in one agile leap, and then danced away, his white tail bobbing.

SOME PLAY *MONOPOLY*, WHILE OTHERS PLAY FARMER

Today, Sarah and Laura played *Monopoly* for the first time. Watching and listening to them I felt nostalgic.

This was a rainy, gray November Sunday. Football was occupying most of the television stations. Little brothers were napping, so getting out a game with lots of little pieces wasn't a problem. I was standing at the ironing board, in the kitchen, available to instruct their first adventure where you're handed $1,500 and given $200 each time you pass "GO."

Within a short time, nine-year-old Laura owned both utilities, all four railroads, Boardwalk and Park Place. Sarah had green and orange properties with houses on them, but the game was in Laura's hands. It was interesting, hearing them trade real estate. They worked out some pretty fair deals. Often Laura would even offer Sarah a big wad of money just to keep her in the game. Finally, after about an hour and a half, Sarah went bankrupt.

The girls ate supper, took baths, and quickly went back to sharpen their real estate prowess. Laura lost game number two. She took it pretty hard. Game number three is already underway.

Board games have a way of getting you hooked. I remember my sisters and I were addicted to *Parcheesi*. We'd play every day after school, our homework often times taking an unfortunate back seat. Too bad we couldn't study *Parcheesi 101* in college.

After a short nap, seven-year-old Scott put on his boots, an old jacket, and went to the barn to play "Farmer". He helped his Dad get stanchions and water cups ready for the heifers that will soon come in for the winter. They were in the barn when thunder and lightning began to roll, making terrific noise. After the sky calmed down, I went down to see how they were coming along. Scott proudly showed me how he'd spread straw on the floor for the heifers to lie on. The barn cats watched with interest. There'll be a lot more activity in the barn when the Holsteins are moved back in from the pasture.

Three-year-old Johnny played the perfect role for himself—a little brother finding innovative ways to annoy the older kids. However in the evening, the four children actually worked in harmony. Their Grandpa Dumas had given Scott a big bag of butternuts. I told the kids that, if they shelled the bag, I'd make fudge.

They went outside. Each of them had individual tasks. It was fun watching their assembly line activities. Scott used his hammer to crack the nuts on the sidewalk. Sarah and Laura used tiny picks to dig out the butternut meat. Johnny's job, which he did with enthusiasm, was to pick up discarded shell pieces and put them in a paper bag.

Judging by the initial size of the bag of whole nuts and comparing the half-cup of nut pieces, I think that maybe Johnny was a little too enthusiastic about his duties. But that's okay. I have a feeling that the fudge will taste great.

I'm sure the girls will be back to Monopoly soon. For now, it's good to see them together outside working as a team.

EIGHT CHILDREN
NOT ALWAYS ENOUGH

My daughters and I stopped at the grocery store after church on Sunday. We needed milk and waffles. I ended with $56 worth of groceries, but forgot the waffles.

At the checkout, I mentioned to the cashier that the music on the PA system was half scratchy static and half Christmas music. I suggested that turning it off would actually be an improvement. To my surprise, she immediately acted on my complaint. She sent another employee to tell the manager. I was glad that the noise was immediately rectified.

I was impressed by the disposition of the checkout woman. I remembered that she'd waited on me before and was unusually friendly. Kindness and consideration flowed from her smile, voice and manner.

When she swung around to put the bags down into my cart, I noticed that she was quite advanced in her pregnancy. I asked when she was due and she answered, "In one week." I thought about when I was pregnant. I always looked for a place to sit down. Standing for long periods of time and handling heavy groceries were not easy tasks.

I asked her, "Isn't it hard for you to be on your feet so much? Isn't it hard loading those bags into the cart?"

She said, "It's not bad, except when I work 7 to 11 in the evening. Then, my back begins to ache, mostly from being tired out from the whole day's activities."

I thought maybe this was going to be her second child, and maybe she could rest while her toddler was napping. So I said, "Can you rest a little during the day so that you won't be so worn out by evening?"

Do you know what she said?

"Well, I have eight children, so I keep pretty busy."

I was floored!

I said, "Are you kidding? You have eight children? You don't look old enough! Are they all yours?"

She thanked me for the compliment, assured me that they were all hers and casually added that they were eight boys. I was astounded. I slapped the counter, and started to laugh.

Here was a happy, friendly, hardworking pregnant woman with eight boys. Can you imagine the laundry, meals, Christmas presents, homework, snacks, haircuts, needs, time, wants, desires, love, fun, noise, moments, memories, relationships, beds and socks in that home?

I said, "Oh, God bless you! What a big family! Wouldn't it be something if you have a girl?"

She smiled and said, "Oh, I'll probably have another boy. Thank you for not making me feel guilty like some people who think I'm overpopulating the world."

I interrupted, "Are you kidding? I applaud you. The world needs more positive productive people like you."

"We have real good boys," she said. And her last statement left me feeling inspired for life. With a lot of conviction, she added, "I have nothing to complain about."

Imagine that!

SMILE

Update: Do you remember in last week's column when I told you about the pregnant lady in the grocery store? Remember that she had eight boys? Guess what! Michael and Lynne Carr and their sons Michael Jr., Mark, Jeffery, Scott, Jamie, Daniel, Jeremy and Timothy are pleased to announce the new baby girl in their lives, Jill Rachel Carr. Alleluia!

GLOW OF CHRISTMAS LASTS A LONG TIME

Christmas is celebrated in so many ways, with beautiful songs, family traditions, joyful greetings, meaningful messages, and people recognizing the bigger picture. A special glow surrounds the season.

My husband, four children and I began what might be a new holiday activity for us. We piled into the car and drove around looking at decorated houses. I was the co-pilot with the list from The Citizen's "Christmas Decoration Tour" on my lap. Greg had already mapped out our route to view the contestants. We started on Kenwood Avenue and stayed mesmerized throughout our travels around Auburn.

As it turns out, Dr. Wester from Kenwood Avenue asked to have his home removed from the list. He won the contest last year and wants other homes to have a chance to win. Actually, though, we are all winners because we get to enjoy the spirit of anyone who puts a wreath on their door or puts a light in their window.

As we drove around the city we appreciated the uniqueness, charm, colors, greenery, red bows, nativity scenes, Santa Clauses, reindeer, snowmen and giant Christmas cards.

There were some unique gifts at our house this year. Sarah and Laura bought their gerbils', Cloudy and Sparky, a metal wheel for the little critters to exercise on. And they bought the tiny guys a vehicle to investigate the world. The gerbils now own an automobile. It's a plastic transparent ball with air holes and a removable top to put the pilot in.

Sparky quickly learned how to operate the "Chevy" and he took off like Mario Andretti. What a riot! His little feet scrambled as he ripped down the stretches, under tables and around corners. When he hit a wall, he turned around and headed in the other direction. We laughed and giggled at their antics. Cloudy was a much slower drive. At one point, he went to sleep at the wheel, so to speak, and just sat there, holding up traffic. Gerbils are quire fundorable (a new word).

The glow of Christmas continued at the YMCA recently. There was a bloodmobile held in Patsy McGinnis's name. I went to give blood, but wasn't allowed because of a shot of Novocain I'd received at the dentist's the day before. But I was still glad that I went. The bustle of activity reminded me of Santa's workshop.

Just picture a large room divided into sections by tables, chairs and volunteers. A person donating blood took about one hour to weave through the different steps. I was impressed by the turnout of donors. What greater gift could there be than the "Gift of Life?" It's a wonderful way to share the meaning of Christmas all year.

And I was also surprised at the number of workers donating their time and energies this busy holiday season.

The room contained a special glow.

ONE OF THOSE AHA MOMENTS

Mind if I write about this age thing? I'll try. I'm only 37. I'm all of 37. I'm *already* 37. I'm very young. I feel very old.

I re-entered the work force after an eleven--year absence. Since returning, I found myself in a whole new environment. I am no longer one of the young technologists. I am middle-aged now. Gray, actually I prefer to say silver, has befriended some hair on my head. In a way, I feel I've earned this silver tinge. It's a distinguished look, demanding wisdom and respect! Then again, it makes me look old. But the color of my hair is not the only sign. There is a serious look that I possess. It is not so much an invited look, but one that just sort of sits on my face and will not leave.

The brown age spots are unsightly, but what can I do? Here's the problem. Inside this dead giveaway, old person is a vibrant, fun-loving, eager, innocent, enthusiastic girl. I am in here. I feel like I always did, except for an early morning backache. I still love life, but my youth feels stuck inside.

I experienced one of those Aha moments. I imagine "this stuck in your body" feeling is universal. I suppose that my seventy-eight-year-old father-in-law feels trapped in his body too. I bet there are many senior citizens and middle-lifers who feel like young foals. Yet they are saddled with the weight of their age.

Options? Color my hair. I tried that, it just wasn't me. I know. I *know*. That was the point right?

Make a conscious effort to smile more, to shake off that serious side? I feel silly. I feel that people look at me and think, "Why does she have that silly look on her face?"

Put make-up on over the age spots? Turns my white uniform orange around the collar.

Let's see, what options are left? Wear a pin that reads: "2 Young, 2 Be, 4 Gotten?" Dumb. Call Ponce de Leon's great grand-children? See if they have any answers. Okay.

I suppose I have to accept this. Appreciate that this is called life and realize that a lot of people feel this way. And try to hang on to that kid in me. Be wise *and* silly, serious *and* fun.

I guess I'll give it a whirl.

LITTLE BOYS ARE MADE UP OF THINGS IN THEIR POCKETS

We can only imagine what our children will grow up to be...

Our three-year-old Johnny has smart godparents! Pat and Richie gave him *Alf* pajamas for Christmas. Johnny thinks Alf is funny and identifies with the furry alien's wacky style. And Barb and Tom gave him *Superman* PJs, complete with red cape. Now, Johnny runs around the house with his arms outstretched. The red cape flaps in the wind behind him. Johnny's two sets of godparents sure pegged his heroes. Who knows? Johnny might be the next super hero.

You want your kids to identify with the "good guys." Alf has a great sense of humor and has some good basic principles except for his diet of kitty-cats. Superman stands for justice and righteousness.

If Johnny turns out somewhere between their ideals, he will be one cool dude.

The other evening I watched our six-year-old son, Scott remove the contents of his right front pocket. When Scott was a little tyke, he was chubby with fat cheeks and, lots of creases and folds on his arms and legs. Over the years, Scott grew taller and thinner. Now at the ripe age of six, he's a long lean machine and his blue jeans hug his frame. I'm surprised when I see him pulling so many prized possessions out of his pocket. How could all those things fit in there? Like a magician pulling rabbits and birds out of a hat, Scott pulled out his duck billed dinosaur. It's green and rubbery. He got the four-inch Trachodon at a birthday party in October. Ever since that day, Scott has kept that rubbery reptile by his side. He holds it when he's sleeping and carries it in his pocket when he is awake.

Next, he pulled out one red and one green bouncy ball. They're each twice the size of a large marble.

A fortune in coins followed: two quarters, one penny, and one fake "Smokey the Bear" half-dollar.

The last treasure, culled from a Rice Krispie's box was his most recent acquisition: a glow-in-the-dark talking skeleton head. It doesn't actually talk, but its mouth moves up and down.

Scott gingerly placed his assets on the chair. For him, carrying all these things around is common practice. Unfortunately, I cannot fit more than a thin dime in some of my jean pockets. Either my jeans are shrinking or I'm… I can't even say it.

Surely we can't see Scott's future occupation by his pocket paraphernalia but don't you think archaeologist comes to mind?

You read and hear about the objects that little boys carry. Seasons often predict the items. In the summer, its pretty stones, in the fall, acorns and butternuts. Fortunately, no live frogs. Yet. Super hero? Archeologist? We'll see...

IT'S IMPORTANT TO KEEP BLAZING NEW TRAILS

I left the Sunday dinner dishes soaking in the dishpan. There was laundry in the hamper, scaling the bathroom wall. A stack of mending stared at me blankly as I looked for my wool socks. There was a lot of housework and paperwork that I could have done, but I was not convinced it was essential. Instead, Sarah, Laura and I went cross-country skiing for about two hours. What a riot! Their excitement and eagerness to learn was inspiring.

Sarah did very well for her second time on skis. She fell about 10 times but made it down the big hill twice without falling. Laura was another story. This was her first time on skis. She fell down a lot in the beginning, about 40 times, but her spirit never faltered. At times, she appeared to be made of rubber. She'd fall, and then bounce right back up. Sometimes, her legs, feet, skis and poles would get tangled in a mess. She'd quickly unravel herself, stand up and exclaim, "Where are the BIG hills?" They both got quite adept by the end of our adventure. I was proud of them.

I was glad that instead of doing mundane chores that day, I went frolicking through the woods with my young daughters. We explored trails, laughed a lot, and built some bridges into the future. Those bridges help on days like today.

Today was not my best day. I woke up late and I hate feeling behind. Usually, I like to prepare for breakfast and organize the day. Since I overslept till 6 a.m., I wasn't able to cushion the morning for our four children. While I was busy fixing their lunches, they had to fix their breakfasts. Then, I cleaned the breakfast table while they looked for their sneakers.

Tensions mounted. Sarah whined loudly to me, "I thought this Blistex would take care of my cold sore. It still hurts." She stared at me like a disgruntled patient about to sue for malpractice. I answered, "Excuse me. I didn't say your cold sore would magically disappear instantly."

I combed Scott's and Johnny's hair and waited impatiently for Laura to get in line. I kept dipping the comb in a cup of hot water to quiet the static electricity in their hair. Laura dawdled and took so long that I yelled, "Okay Laura, you've got to comb your own hair!" And I slammed the comb down. Laura picked up the comb and mistakenly put it in a nearby cup of milk.

My fuse shortened. Why couldn't these kids get their act together?

I dropped a log on my foot and spilled a glass of water on the kitchen floor. I dropped a whole egg, shell and all, in the buttery frying pan. Then, it dawned on me. I'm not so perfect either. I was the one who overslept. Why was I expecting so much from everybody else?

I decided these difficult moments are when bridges come in handy. We need to keep taking time out for fun, blazing new trails. We've found our way out of the woods before with shared enthusiasm. I'm sure we'll do it again and again.

TRIBUTE TO A
WOMAN I NEVER KNEW

(Stephanie Sroka Panek 1920-1965)

I was cleaning out the dresser in my father-in-law's room and found a hairbrush, comb, mirror, and some bobby-pins in the small center drawer. The dresser was my mother-in-law's. I never met her. She died 12 years before I married her son, too soon at the age of 45.

I've heard a lot about her. I imagined a gentle, thoughtful mother who was hard-working but enjoyed it. She loved gardening and gladiolus. She milked cows, raised chickens, picked berries, made jam, built shelves in cupboards, won a Pillsbury award, painted the outside of our big farmhouse, chopped wood, was a great cook, and was devoted to her family.

When I married Greg, I was sad that I could never know his mother. I think we would have liked each other.

Now here was her hairbrush with her soft, brown/gray hair woven in the bristles. I stopped in awe. This was a link to the past and I relished the opportunity for me to feel close to this person I could not meet.

When I raised the brush to my face to get a closer look, I could smell the unmistakable odor of oils from her hair. I stood still, smelling the brush, fingering the hair, and got a deeper sense of this woman who graced the earth for too short a time.

She seems more real to me now. Unlike photographs or anecdotes, this was part of her. She had used this brush like so many of the things in this house. However, the other things she used, like the electric mixer or the canning jars, are not as personal.

I didn't share my treasure with anyone. I was unsure of how my husband and father-in-law would react. I was worried they might think me silly or even morbid. Eventually, I washed the brush and comb and put them in the bathroom vanity.

I thought of keeping the strands of hair, but I know that you can't hang on to everything. Besides, I'll always remember the closeness that I felt for Mom Panek then. I'll remember her warm, honest, sincere scent. And I'm happy for that.

The anniversary of her birth is Feb. 11, close to Valentine's Day and close to our hearts.

BEING HUNGRY IS NO PICNIC

Tonight after supper and dishes, I sat at the table. I was keeping half an ear on the 6 o'clock news, drinking a cup of coffee and reading a magazine.

My youngest son, Johnny, was standing on a kitchen chair next to me. He was sort of combing my hair while he chattered away.

The article that I was reading was about Medjugorje, a small mountain village in Yugoslavia. The blessed Mother of Jesus has been appearing there to six young adults, for seven years.

The account was interesting, inspiring, and reassuring. While I was reading, Johnny suddenly slipped. His leg went down between our two chairs. He didn't get hurt, but the table got jostled and my coffee spilled onto the magazine. I wiped it up, but a brown circle remained. The circle was about one-inch in diameter. I looked at the printed words made visible by the brown smudge:

"Pray more deeply

"Messages are peace

"Prayer and fasting
"connected. If we live these
"will understand"

I was in awe. Out of the 10-page article, these coffee-stained words contained the gist of the whole story.

After some thought, I decided to try fasting. I'm apprehensive. I enjoy eating as much as most people. But the odd thing is, we recently had two families over to play *Pictionary*. We had a lot of fun, a lot of laughs and a lot of food. Of course, we were celebrating being together and had more refreshments than necessary. At one point, I looked around the table. There were assorted nuts, chips, vegetables, dips, and drinks. We'd all eaten supper a few hours earlier, yet here we were eating as a social habit. It seemed unfair to all people who are really hungry for affluent people to treat food this way.

Fasting is foreign to me. However, being a writer, I thought I'd share my observations while fasting. I'll try it out and provide journal entries to tell you how I fare.

Just writing those words I feel starved already.

Following Day: 6:15 a.m., made coffee, set the breakfast table and then went upstairs. I was just thinking about people with eating disorders. I wouldn't want anyone to fast if there is a medical reason why they shouldn't.

8:10 a.m. I'm hungry. My stomach keeps giving me sounds and sensations that it wants something to eat. However, I'm not in pain. I'm not dizzy. I don't have a headache. I left the kitchen while my husband ate. Then I fixed waffles/syrup for Scott, scrambled eggs for the girls, oatmeal for Johnny, and lunches for the kids to take to school. It all smelled so good.

The good news is I'm getting a lot accomplished, and have a lot of energy. My stomach is keeping my mind grounded as to why I'm doing this. It's a form of prayer.

9:15 a.m. a hot cup of herbal tea which was wonderful.

10:45 a.m. I'm so hungry my stomach is squeaking. I realize many people don't eat breakfast but it's my favorite meal.

Johnny and I went outside. We picked up what my neighbor would call squaw wood (fallen limbs and sticks). Don't know if exercise was such a good idea but frankly I've been busy all morning.

I'm tempted to eat. I don't enjoy this feeling. It's uncomfortable. If I quit this fast then either you'll know it or I just won't have a column for this week.

I'm going to see this through. I'm curious about its worth.

12:30 p.m. made it through lunch. A neighbor stopped by. She mentioned that she recently fasted and seeing her alive and well meant it *could* be done.

3:15 p.m. slight headache.

Interesting conversation today about how we are polluting the earth, what we are doing to the ozone layer, about the millions killed by Hitler's commands.

I don't know what I'm to learn from this no eating day. Except now I feel sad for people who are hungry every day. I wonder if people in all walks of life fasted, once a week, if there would be more compassion, more soul-searching.

4:45 p.m. real headache now. Took two aspirins.

6 p.m. staring at the clock, thinking about going to bed early, getting up early tomorrow, then eating a lot of food. (I'm acutely aware that I may eat tomorrow and that I have an abundance of foods to choose from.)

7 p.m. one cup of coffee, I feel more awake yet weak.

What have I learned? All day I had the option to eat a wide variety of foods. Many people don't have that option. There are more hours in the day when you fast. It's not fun being hungry.

Its 8:30 p.m. I'm going to bed soon. I look forward to tomorrow.

Once again I look at the coffee stained words:

"Pray more deeply

"Messages are peace

"Prayer and fasting

"connected. If we live these

"will understand"

FASTING HINTS AND
BROOKS ARE COOL

After my "fasting day" last week, I've learned some dos and don'ts.

Eat light the night before.

On the day of the "fast," drink lots of water and some fruit juice.

Eat some fruit for energy.

Do not drink caffeinated beverages.

Introduce foods slowly the next day.

The old saying, "Learn something new every day" seems to fit here. If fasting is done properly, I can see its benefits. Being hungry makes you more aware. It sharpens your senses and teaches you to appreciate more.

*****

Are you having a hard time remembering the season? It sure has acted like spring most of this month of January. The kids and I went for a long walk around our farm this weekend. Our travels took us over corn, wheat, and hayfields. We made our way through hedges and had the most fun by the brooks and the pond.

We enjoyed looking at the delicate ice formations and were mesmerized by the cold deep water.

IS THAT A FLY OR A SNOWMOBILE IN MY EAR?

It was just about a year ago. I sat up in bed, a wreck. My brain was trying to comprehend. My fragile mind at 4 a.m. was torn, fragmented. Within one-second, I knew the horrible truth. I was not dreaming. There was a fly in my ear. I shook my husband and whispered a scream, "Greg, wake up. There's a fly in my ear!" Naturally, Greg was rattled and not coherent. I was on the brink of insanity. I shook him awake and he followed my mad gallop into the bathroom. My conscious mind recalled a science fiction movie about a worm that permeated the brain of someone and started eating his brain and deranging his mind.

At the end of the movie, the surgeon told the patient with the invading worm that he had successfully removed the parasite. Upon removal the surgeon discovered that the worm was female and had recently laid her eggs.

I violently pushed these horrendously vivid thoughts out of my mind, knowing if I dwelled on them I just might slip to the other side of sanity.

I turned on the bright overhead light in the bathroom and, as Greg blinked awake, I was dancing around, screaming, lunging, and feeling faint and hysterical.

Back while I was in bed, after I'd realized the stark reality, I had put my finger in my ear hoping to pull the beast out. My efforts had merely pushed him in further.

Now, under the bright clinical bathroom light, I could feel the winged creature rotate inside my ear. It buzzed as it moved.

Greg, finally able to think, grabbed me, put his mouth on my ear and began to suck. Now, my emotions were really twisted. I would have undergone any treatment in the world to liberate this monster from inside my ear but the rationale of Greg, in his tighty--whities, sucking on my ear like a vacuum cleaner was almost too much for me and for a split second I had to squelch the urge to laugh.

My mind flirted with the idea of Greg succeeding in sucking the fly out of my ear and it lying victoriously in his mouth, but I was too trapped in the cold hard facts to entertain this picture.

When the mouth to ear method failed, Greg suggested that I hit the side of my head with my hand while stomping on one foot. I quickly followed his orders and jumped fervently on my right foot while pounding the right side of my head. It worked! I could feel the mini chainsaw walk to the precipice of my ear's opening and fly away.

I have never been the same. I slept very little after that. It was hard to breathe way down under the covers.

For nights and days I was tormented by this true nightmare. Every fly after that was a potential slayer of my sanity.

Finally, I began to accept the incident unlikely to reoccur and convinced myself to go on with my life. My story could end here, but it can't. Something happened about a week later.

To be continued...

MECHANICAL FLY SPOILS ONENESS WITH NATURE

Remember last week I told you about the fly in my ear that I finally liberated by banging the side of my head? Something similar happened one week later.

A glorious, sunny, wintry Sunday arrived. We ate a good dinner, the children took a nap, my husband split wood, and my father-in-law sat by the wood-burning stove. I grabbed the opportunity to relish my favorite winter activity. Quickly, I dressed in warm clothes, put on my boots, locked them into my cross-country skis and flew across the yard to glide and frolic on the reflective, snowy slopes. I was so eager, so expectant, looking forward to the peace of the land and sounds of nature.

My nerves were still fraught from the fly incident and I needed this retreat. While skiing the other day I was overjoyed to discover that the chattering noise above me was a family of squirrels. Each time out on skis, I am able to free myself from the chains of motherhood. I forget about housework and soar with the wind. I love the sound of my skies as they sing and whistle and the sounds that the snow makes as it creaks and bends to accommodate me.

Just as I neared the pond and began my peaceful stride in winter's beauty, my recently ravaged right ear began to twitch with a familiar uncomfortable feeling. My tranquility began to unravel as my eyes scanned the horizon. There, like a flyspeck on a distant hill, was a buzzing snowmobile.

By nature, I am a peaceful person. I'm easy-going, I like harmony, and I don't like confrontation. But the horror of the fly in my ear had resurfaced. Speeding toward my ski path was a loud, obnoxious trespasser.

I thought about turning around and going home, knowing that I could not share my space with this intruder. But I just could not give in. This land was ours! This was my peaceful Sunday! This was war.

At right angles, we sped toward a favorite spot of mine. You need to ski down into a hollow, over a creek bed, up the narrow wooded trail to the peacefulness of this secluded field.

The snowmobile and rider zoomed past me with a high-pitched whine and then turned around to follow me into the hollow. I stopped at the top of the field, turned, and waited for the masked rider. Part of me was afraid. I was a girl alone in a secluded field--no houses near. Here was a stranger following me. However, the part of me that usually stays dormant and silent was outraged. The noise and insistence of this machine brought me back to recent memories.

I stood there, hoping that the person would stop as I had. Instead, he zipped right past me with a whining, roaring sound, making it totally impossible for me to hear any birds, squirrels or rustling corn stalks.

The fly like creature went way down to the end of the field. My hopes of being rid of him were dashed when I realized that he had turned around and was heading toward me at full speed.

We were sharing the same trail. As I was skiing south, he was zooming north. To him, this was a game--sort of like "chicken." Who would move out of the way first? I stood my ground. Just as he pivoted his trespassing, noise-polluting, fly on skis off the trail, to go around me, I used my ski pole as a giant fly swatter and whacked him on the rear! Finally I got his attention. He stopped the droning machine and yelled, "What'd you do that for?"

I yelled, "No one gave you permission to be on this land!"

He quickly turned the key and sped off. Perhaps he'd been pretending that he owned this land, paid our taxes, and that I was on his domain. He buzzed away.

I could finally hear the wind.

HOW I TRAVELED AROUND THE WORLD TRYING TO GET BACK HOME

I probably sounded like Helen Reddy saying, "I am woman, hear me roar!" My four children, husband, and father-in-law were concerned about me. I planned to go up north by myself for my mother's retirement dinner and had to convince them that I'd be fine.

This column is not going to be about how proud I am of my mother though she worked for 24 years for the Franklin County Community Action Agency and was its director for the past nine years. The party Friday night attended by 150 people, the speeches and the tributes, the fact that her eight daughters surprised her by coming from Arizona, Washington D.C., Albany, Auburn, Massena, and Saranac Lake--all of that was so special! But this column isn't going to be about Mom's accomplishments.

Nor will I write about my seven sisters though they are all tall and gorgeous, individuals with special gifts and talents. I won't carry on about them, their handsome husbands, or their sweet children.

Instead, I will write about how I traveled around the world to get to my hometown. I'm pretty cocky about traveling. Back in the early 1970s, a girlfriend and I traveled in her van across the United States. We took six months, weaving across the country. We picked lemons in Yuma, Arizona, for one day. That experience was a wake-up call! We worked as waitresses for two months, and then meandered through the States and came back to New York. So you see I am a seasoned traveler. Finding my way around--it's a no— brain-er.

The route to my hometown of Malone is firmly etched in my mind: Weedsport, Thruway, Syracuse, 81 North, Watertown, Route 11B north, and Malone. Simple.

I headed out Friday morning, reassuring my family, "Don't worry, I'll be fine. See you Sunday."

With seat buckle on, sun shining, radio playing soft rock, I got on the Thruway. My mind was on my parents and my sisters and what I'd say to each of them. I felt so free and happy, independent and relaxed.

Then suddenly, I felt very confused. Where the heck was I? How come I wasn't seeing signs for Watertown? How come I was seeing signs for Utica, Amsterdam, and Schenectady?

Without looking down at the seat next to me, my hand felt for the Thruway ticket. A horrible pain in the pit of my gut came over me. I didn't want to accept the truth—that I was still on the Thruway. I had not taken the Syracuse exit. I was not on 81 north.

Watertown was not ahead of me, Albany was! It was as though I'd been traveling in a time warp. My mind was on so many wonderful thoughts, I was singing to the radio, loving the freedom, passing big tractor trailers, missing my exit!

I wanted to pull off to the side of the road, crawl into the fetal position and just stay there. Surely, tears would help at a time like this? But only wails, groans and moans poured out of me. I was yelling at myself—missing out on so much time with family. It felt like eons before I got to the next exit.

The lady at the tollbooth was sweet. Perhaps she noticed the anguished look on my face and knew she was dealing with a fragile mind. She said, "Oh dear. No problem. Just turn around, drive back twenty miles, get off in Utica, and take Route 12 to Watertown." I paid the exorbitant toll of $2.90 and meekly turned my pickup truck around to revisit the scenes of my nightmare. I couldn't tell how much time would be added to my travels, but I knew that it was going to make for a long day.

I thought I was in the Netherlands. I went through towns called Copenhagen, Stockholm, Denmark. I went past a Bass shoe outlet, if you ever wondered where one was.

When I finally got to Watertown, I called my husband. I said, "Don't worry, everything's fine. I left home four hours ago, I should be in Malone, but I'm in Watertown. It was sort of like the Bermuda Triangle! I'll call you when I get to Malone."

By the time I got to Potsdam, the back of my neck felt like a jammed cable. I pulled over to the Edge of Town Diner and ordered coffee to go. I popped two Bufferin into my mouth (after removing my foot) and headed north once again. I burned my tongue on the coffee and spilled some on my coat, but when I turned the dial on the radio and heard people talking French from the Canadian stations, I knew I was almost home.

The four--hour trip took six and 1/2 hours, but the lesson in humility was probably good for me.

Why am I telling you all of this? If you did something stupid today, maybe you won't feel quite so bad.

NEVER A DULL MOMENT
BUYING GROCERIES

It was a Wednesday and there wasn't any school. We needed to get groceries and I decided to bring my four children with me. I like getting their input on the food we eat. Plus, I wanted them to see people and sights, you know, to broaden their scope of the world around us. So, off we went to Wegmans in quest of enough groceries to feed seven people for seven days.

Sarah pushed Johnny in one cart. Laura and Scott walked with me while I pushed another cart. After getting toothpaste, breads and chocolate cookies, we chose our produce and fruit. Next we casually pushed our baskets to the meat department, unaware of the pending doom.

I was in search of the roast beef on sale. Thought I'd get two big roasts, enough for leftovers. As we approached the beef section,

I stood next to an elderly woman who was deciding which package to choose. I patiently gazed over her shoulder, eyeing what I would pick when she moved on.

Suddenly, a towering presence loomed over us. With lunging body movements of forceful swinging hips, a tall woman with bleached blonde hair and broad shoulders rudely pushed us aside. The older woman and I shot each other side-glances. We were both disgusted with this Roller Derby Queen. The queen with the big hips moved many containers of meat before finding the four biggest choices of beef roasts. As she swung around, balancing her trophies in her arms, I muttered very loudly, "Exc-u-u-u-u-se me!"

As the Derby Queen strode to her short, wimpy gray-haired husband and daughter waiting at their cart, the older woman and I spoke of how rude some people are.

While Lady Goliath was tossing the meat into her cart, she loudly ranted, "Some people have all the time in the world to grocery shop!"

Ut--oh. That struck a nerve with me!

I marched over to the bleached blonde and said, "Excuse me, but I have four children and I happen to have a very busy day today and I don't have a lot of time to grocery shop!"

She haughtily put her big, bold face very close to mine and snarled, "Well then, you'd better get to work!"

For lack of the perfect reply, I responded, "I don't think you're very nice."

She then shouted, "Bullshit!" and started to lead her husband and daughter away.

My children were fascinated with the scenario. I was so angry I grabbed the elderly woman's arm and said, "Can you believe her?"

Together, the old lady and I glared at the towering inferno. She shot a final insult at us: "Stick it up you're a--!"

Well, I'll tell ya, my children's scope of the world was broadened that day. They saw and heard things that will certainly enlighten them forever.

SPRING: MUSIC AND COLOR AND FRAGRANCE

Spring's almost here and there's music in the air. So what's all this fuss about longer days? Granted the aroma of the grass, trees, and breeze lift you off the ground. The air is practically intoxicating--but it's only fresh, clean, fragrant air.

Crocuses will soon jump out of the soil. They'll lie low and still and make no sound, except for the music produced in your heart when you see their delicate yellow and purple flowers.

The trees are getting ready to shout as they release their new leaf buds. That's significant. I mean they've had bare branches silhouetted against the cold winter skies and now are beginning to fill in. Each tree is starting anew.

Before you know it, forsythia bushes will serenade us with magnificent yellow sounds. Her bright branches will soothe our weary eyes. Hyacinths will ring like hundreds of bells, daffodils will shout, and tulips will join in with melodious voices.

But what's the big deal? It's just the song of spring in a symphony of nature. It's just the flowing brooks and happy sounds of birds. It's just kids on bikes and metal swings being oiled. It's just the sound of tractors pulling plows and the flutter of seagulls flocking on the dark brown earth. Ask any farmer how good it is to plow the field after the long winter's chill.

Better yet, watch his bouncy gait as he heads for the tool shed to saddle up his John Deere. So what if spring brings abundant new life, promise and hope? It's just a season.

It's just a change. It's just filled with music, color and fragrance.

It's just cleansing rain for the earth to drink, days getting longer, warmer, and sweeter. It's just for fishing, gardening, walking, skipping, running, splashing in puddles, and picking forget-me-nots. Perhaps falling in love?

It's just probably the absolute best time of the year. But we all know that. So, what's the big deal?

PRAYING ROSARY BECOMES
A FORM OF BONDING

Tonight my nine-year-old daughter Laura and I did something different. We prayed the rosary together. It was great. From 7:35 to 7:55 p.m., we prayed the Glorious Mysteries and it was indeed glorious. At one point during our prayer, we sat and smiled at each other, our hearts merging.

We prayed for a teenage girl who is faced with abortion but choose to enter a home for unwed mothers. We prayed that Laura and her sister and brothers would be strong and mindful of their friendships. We prayed for the kid's schoolwork and that our relationship will grow and flourish.

Perhaps it sounds too personal to relate this. Perhaps you're uncomfortable discussing prayer or thinking about it. But it's so rewarding. I don't want to silence the feeling.

Two days passed… Laura and I have prayed the rosary for three days in a row. It's bonding for us. I appreciate and savor this time. Scott prayed with us last night and Sarah joined us tonight. All too quickly, the kids will be grown up and out on their own. We all have memories. What will those memories be?

Praying makes us more conscious of the present. Everything that we do say, eat, drink, smoke, think, or write has some small effect on our future. Little decisions can be as significant as big ones. Praying helps us to direct our thoughts.

Can't describe how good it felt tonight when I asked 11-year-old Sarah what intentions she wanted to pray for. She thought for a while and said, "There's so many. For the poor, for child abuse, to make bad people good, so that kids in school will stop picking on this one kid, so that Patsy McGinnis, who had another liver transplant will get better." We prayed for all of those intentions and our hearts felt better.

Saying the rosary is just one form of prayer and is probably foreign to a lot of people. Reading the Bible, going to church, talking to God, are other ways of spending memorable time with your youngsters or teenager.

I'm not proclaiming that my family and I are perfect, of course. But I don't always want to write about spilled milk here. What's the point? There's so much negative in the news already. I'm just as human as you are. I sin, make mistakes, and screw up. My parenting skills fall short. I scream, yell, and carry on like a normal neurotic mom. However, when I try something, see its significance and feel its balm, I want to share the good news.

P.S. Unfortunately, my column has been eliminated. So, this is farewell.

My thanks to The Citizen for allowing me to express my thoughts. And thanks to you, readers, for listening.

God Bless.

About the Author

Bobbie's first book, *Morning Walks: zen meditations* published by FootHills Publishing, uncovers subtle, seasonal changes on her two-mile walk to work. Her articles were published in the magazines *Birds and Blooms*, *Reminisce Extra*, Empire State College's literary journal, *Many Waters*, and in Father's Shamon's book, *The Power of the Rosary*. Her poetry was in the anthology, *Common Intuitions*, in Moondance, aaduna, and The National League of American Pen Women on-line magazines and her poetry will be included in two upcoming anthologies with the NLAPW: *The Light Between Us* and *The Super Moon*. Bobbie also wrote blogs for the Cayuga County Tourism Office website, participated in numerous poetry readings in central and western New York, and was a judge for the CNY Pen Women Award for Poetry Contest, and for the Skaneateles High School's Poetry Out Loud Contest.

www.bobbiedumaspanek.com

Made in the USA
Middletown, DE
30 September 2015